NAPLES TRAVEL GUIDE 2025

Your Ultimate Companion to Exploring History, Culture, and Coastal Beauty in Italy's Vibrant City

ARIA WILD

Copyright © 2024 by Aria Wild

All rights reserved. No part of this publication may be reproduced, distributed, or transmitted in any form or by any means, including photocopying, recording, or other electronic or mechanical methods, without the prior written permission of the publisher, except in the case of brief quotations embodied in critical reviews and certain other noncommercial uses permitted by copyright law. For permission requests, please contact the publisher.

Published by Aria Wild

1600 DOC NICHOLS RD

Durham NC, U.S.A

Cover design by Rodriguez Mitchell

Interior design by Rodriguez Mitchell

Maps by Gabriel Chapman

Editing by Aria Wild

Typesetting by Aria Wild

Photographs by Aria Wild

Printed in U.S.A

TABLE OF CONTENTS

INTRODUCTION 5
   WELCOME TO NAPLES 5
   WHY VISIT NAPLES IN 2025 7
   HOW TO USE THIS GUIDE 11
CHAPTER ONE 17
   PLANNING YOUR TRIP 17
      BEST TIMES TO VISIT NAPLES 17
      ENTRY REQUIREMENTS AND VISAS 20
      GETTING TO NAPLES 23
      TRANSPORTATION 28
CHAPTER TWO 35
   GETTING AROUND NAPLES 35
      PUBLIC TRANSPORT 35
      WALKING AND EXPLORING NEIGHBOURHOODS.39
      CAR RENTALS AND DRIVING TIPS 45
CHAPTER THREE 52
   WHERE TO STAY 52
      BEST NEIGHBOURHOODS FOR VISITORS 52
      LUXURY HOTELS AND RESORTS 59
      MID-RANGE AND BOUTIQUE ACCOMMODATIONS 64
      BUDGET-FRIENDLY OPTIONS 71
CHAPTER FOUR 78
   TOP ATTRACTIONS AND LANDMARKS 78
      THE HISTORIC CENTER OF NAPLES 78
      NAPLES CATHEDRAL 85
      CASTEL DELL'OVO AND CASTEL NUOVO 91
      PIAZZA DEL PLEBISCITO AND ROYAL PALACE 96
CHAPTER FIVE 104
   CULTURAL AND HISTORICAL HIGHLIGHTS 104
      ARCHAEOLOGICAL MUSEUM OF NAPLES 104
      SAN GREGORIO ARMENO 113
      TEATRO DI SAN CARLO 118
      LOCAL ART AND CONTEMPORARY GALLERIES 124
CHAPTER SIX 133
   FOOD AND CULINARY EXPERIENCES 133
      THE BIRTHPLACE OF PIZZA 133
      TRADITIONAL NEAPOLITAN CUISINE 139
      STREET FOOD AND LOCAL MARKETS 146
      FINE DINING AND WINE EXPERIENCES 153
CHAPTER SEVEN 161
   SHOPPING IN NAPLES 161
      UNIQUE BOUTIQUES AND ARTISAN SHOPS 161
      EXPLORING VIA TOLEDO AND LOCAL MARKETS 169
      SOUVENIRS AND MUST-HAVE KEEPSHAKES 176
CHAPTER EIGHT 184

NATURE AND OUTDOOR ADVENTURES 184
    MOUNT VESUVIUS 184
    NAPLES BAY AND THE AMALFI COAST 189
    DAY TRIPS TO CAPRI, ISCHIA, AND PROCIDA 193
    PARKS AND GARDENS IN THE CITY 197
CHAPTER NINE 204
    NIGHTLIFE AND OUTDOOR ADVENTURES 204
    BARS AND APERTIVO SPOTS 204
    LIVE MUSIC AND JAZZ CLUBS 210
    THEATERS AND CULTURAL EVENTS 217
CHAPTER TEN 226
    DAY TRIPS AND EXCURSION 226
    POMPEII AND HERCULANEUM 226
    SORRENTO AND THE AMALFI COAST 232
    EXPLORING CASERTA AND ITS ROYAL PALACE 239
    WINERY TOURS IN CAMPANIA 245
CHAPTER ELEVEN 251
    PRACTICAL TIPS FOR TRAVELERS 251
    HEALTH AND SAFETY IN NAPLES 251
    BUDGETING AND CURRENCY TIPS 258
    NAVIGATING NAPLES AS A SOLO TRAVELER 266
    ESSENTIAL APPS AND RESOURCES 275
CHAPTER TWELVE 280
    NAPLES IN 2025: WHAT'S NEW? 280
    UPCOMING EVENTS AND FESTIVALS 280
    EMERGING TRAVEL TRENDS 287
    SUSTAINABILITY AND ECO-TOURISM 295
ACKNOWLEGDEMENT 303
    ABOUT THE AUTHOR 303

INTRODUCTION

WELCOME TO NAPLES

Welcome to Naples, a city where history, culture, and vibrant life come together in a unique blend. Nestled along the stunning Bay of Naples and framed by the majestic Mount Vesuvius, this ancient city offers an unforgettable experience that combines the allure of its rich past with the energy of modern Italian life.

As you step into Naples, you're entering a place that has been continuously inhabited for over 2,000 years. From the narrow, bustling streets of the historic center to the tranquil views of the Mediterranean, every corner holds a story. Naples is home to world-renowned landmarks like the ancient ruins of Pompeii and Herculaneum, the grand Royal Palace, and the iconic Castel dell'Ovo. But it's not just about monuments it's about the people, the food, and the rhythm of the city that makes it come alive.

Indulge in the flavors of the birthplace of pizza, explore hidden churches, and stroll through lively markets. Whether you're savoring a cup of Neapolitan espresso, gazing over the bay at sunset, or admiring the works of Renaissance masters, Naples offers something for every traveler.

Get ready to immerse yourself in the warmth and authenticity of a city that welcomes you with open arms. Whether you're here for a short visit or a longer stay, Naples promises to leave you with lasting memories and a deeper appreciation for its timeless charm. Welcome to Naples – a place where every moment feels like a new discovery.

WHY VISIT NAPLES IN 2025

Visiting Naples in 2025 offers an exciting opportunity to explore a city rich in history, culture, and natural beauty. As one of the oldest continuously inhabited cities in the world, Naples invites travelers to immerse themselves in its fascinating past, vibrant local life, and iconic landmarks. Whether you're a history buff, a foodie, or an adventurer, Naples in 2025 promises an unforgettable experience.

Naples is renowned for its historical significance. The city's historic center, a UNESCO World Heritage site, is a labyrinth of narrow streets, ancient churches, and monumental buildings that reflect over 2,000 years of history. Famous archaeological sites like Pompeii and Herculaneum offer a unique window into ancient Roman life, preserved by the eruption of Mount Vesuvius in AD 79. The Royal Palace, Castel dell'Ovo, and other stunning architectural treasures are scattered throughout the city, showcasing Naples' evolution from ancient times to the modern era.

For many, Naples is synonymous with pizza, as the city is the birthplace of this world-famous dish. A visit in 2025 provides the perfect opportunity to taste authentic Neapolitan pizza, prepared with fresh ingredients and centuries-old recipes. Whether it's a classic Margherita or a more inventive variety, Naples' pizzerias are an essential part of the city's culinary identity. But the city offers much more than pizza. Naples is also known for its rich pastries, like sfogliatella, and strong coffee culture, offering a full spectrum of culinary delights for food lovers.

Natural beauty surrounds Naples, making it an ideal destination for outdoor enthusiasts. Mount Vesuvius, one of the most famous active volcanoes in the world, offers incredible hiking opportunities and panoramic views of the Gulf of

Naples. Just a short distance away, the Amalfi Coast presents dramatic cliffs, picturesque villages, and stunning coastal vistas. Visitors can also take a boat trip to the nearby Isle of Capri, known for its crystal-clear waters and breathtaking landscapes. Naples serves as the perfect base for exploring these scenic wonders.

The city's cultural scene is rich and diverse, with world-class museums and galleries. The Naples National Archaeological Museum houses one of the most significant collections of Roman artifacts, many of which come from Pompeii and Herculaneum. The Capodimonte Museum, located in a former royal palace, features Italian Renaissance and Baroque masterpieces. In 2025, Naples will continue to host a variety of art exhibitions, music festivals, and cultural events that reflect the city's dynamic creative spirit.

Naples is also known for its lively atmosphere. Its streets are full of energy, with markets, street vendors, and local cafes contributing to the city's vibrant daily life. The neighborhoods of Spaccanapoli and Chiaia offer a perfect mix of traditional charm and modern elegance, where visitors can shop, dine, and experience the rhythm of local life. Naples is a city where people are proud of their heritage and eager to share it with visitors, making it a warm and welcoming place to explore.

In addition to its historical and cultural attractions, Naples is an excellent starting point for exploring the surrounding region. The Amalfi Coast, Caserta Palace, and the ancient ruins of Paestum are all easily accessible from Naples, making it a convenient base for day trips. The city's location on the coast also makes it a perfect launchpad for cruising or taking ferries to nearby islands.

The city has also made strides in sustainable tourism, focusing on preserving its cultural heritage and enhancing its environmental practices. Visitors in 2025 can expect a cleaner, more eco-friendly Naples, with a focus on responsible tourism and the protection of its natural and historical resources.

Whether visiting in the spring when the weather is mild, in summer for the bustling energy of the high season, or in autumn when the region's harvest is celebrated, Naples offers year-round appeal. In 2025, the city's unique blend of history, culture, art, food, and natural beauty makes it an unmissable destination for anyone looking to experience the best of Italy.

HOW TO USE THIS GUIDE

This guide to Naples in 2025 is designed to help you plan an unforgettable visit to one of Italy's most dynamic and historic cities. It provides everything you need, from key attractions to practical tips, allowing you to make the most of your time in Naples.

Start with the Introduction to Naples and Welcome to Naples sections to get a sense of the city's history, atmosphere, and what makes it so unique. These sections set the tone for your visit, introducing Naples' mix of ancient charm, vibrant local life, and stunning coastal beauty.

Explore the Top Attractions to discover the iconic landmarks, historical sites, and natural wonders that Naples has to offer. Highlights include historic landmarks such as the Royal Palace and Castel dell'Ovo, world-famous archaeological sites like Pompeii, Herculaneum, and Mount Vesuvius, and stunning natural beauty such as the Amalfi Coast and the Isle of Capri. Use this section as your sightseeing checklist and prioritize the places that interest you most.

For food lovers, the Food and Drink section is essential. Naples is the birthplace of pizza, and tasting an authentic Neapolitan pizza is a must-do experience. You'll also find recommendations for local specialties, such as sfogliatella pastries, fresh seafood, and the city's rich coffee culture. This section will help you plan meals at legendary pizzerias and explore the culinary treasures that Naples is known for.

Naples is surrounded by extraordinary destinations that are perfect for day trips. Refer to the Day Trips section for inspiration on visiting nearby attractions like the Amalfi Coast, the royal palace at Caserta, or the beautiful Isle of Capri. Use this information to complement your time in the city with memorable excursions.

When planning the timing of your visit, consult the Best Time to Visit section. Spring and autumn offer the best weather with fewer crowds, while summer is ideal for enjoying coastal adventures. Knowing what to expect during each season will help you prepare accordingly.

To ensure smooth and stress-free travel, check the Getting Around and Travel Tips sections. These include practical advice on public transportation, walking through the city's historic streets, and using taxis or rideshare services. You'll also find helpful tips for staying safe, communicating with locals, and respecting local customs.

Finding the perfect place to stay is made easier with the Where to Stay section. Whether you prefer the bustling energy of the historic center, the stylish elegance of Chiaia, or the scenic views of Vomero, there's a neighborhood to match every traveler's needs.

Take time to enjoy Naples' vibrant cultural life by keeping an eye on festivals, events, and exhibitions happening during your visit. Annual celebrations like the Festa di San Gennaro offer an authentic glimpse into the city's traditions, while art and music festivals reflect its dynamic creative spirit.

For sustainable travelers, Naples is increasingly focused on preserving its cultural heritage and natural resources. This guide encourages responsible travel by supporting local businesses, respecting historical sites, and choosing eco-friendly options wherever possible.

This guide is flexible and allows you to personalize your experience. Whether you're drawn to history, art, food, or natural landscapes, Naples has something for everyone. Create an itinerary that suits your travel style, budget, and timeframe, and let this guide serve as your companion for discovering the best that Naples has to offer.

With its rich history, world-class cuisine, stunning scenery, and lively spirit, Naples in 2025 promises to be an unforgettable destination. Use this guide to plan a trip full of discovery, authentic experiences, and lasting memories. Buon viaggio!

CHAPTER ONE

PLANNING YOUR TRIP

BEST TIMES TO VISIT NAPLES

The best times to visit Naples are during the spring (April to June) and autumn (September to October) when the weather is mild, the crowds are manageable, and the city's charm is at its peak. During these months, Naples offers ideal conditions for sightseeing, outdoor adventures, and enjoying its rich cultural and culinary offerings.

Spring in Naples brings pleasant temperatures, typically ranging between 15°C (59°F) and 25°C (77°F), with blooming flowers and clear skies. It's a perfect time to explore the city's landmarks, such as the historic center, Pompeii, and Mount Vesuvius, without the intense summer heat. Cafés spill out onto the streets, markets buzz with local life, and coastal areas like the Amalfi Coast and the island of Capri are particularly beautiful during this season.

Autumn offers similarly comfortable weather, with temperatures ranging from 18°C (64°F) to 26°C (79°F) and fewer tourists compared to the summer months. The air is crisp and clear, making it a great time for hiking Vesuvius, visiting archaeological sites, or taking day trips along the coast. Autumn is also harvest season in the surrounding Campania region, which means an abundance of fresh produce, local festivals, and a chance to enjoy the region's wines and cuisine at their best.

Summer (July and August) is the busiest and hottest time of year in Naples, with temperatures often exceeding 30°C (86°F). While the city can feel crowded, especially around major tourist sites, summer is an excellent time for coastal trips, enjoying Naples' beaches, and exploring the nearby islands of Capri, Ischia, and Procida. If visiting in summer, it's best to plan activities in the early morning or evening to avoid the midday heat. This season also sees a lively calendar of festivals, open-air concerts, and events, adding a vibrant atmosphere to the city.

Winter (November to March) is the quietest time to visit Naples, with fewer crowds and cooler temperatures ranging between 8°C (46°F) and 15°C (59°F). While some coastal areas may be less active, the city itself remains lively and full of charm. Winter is a great time to explore museums, churches, and archaeological sites at a relaxed pace. Naples is particularly beautiful during the Christmas season, with festive lights, elaborate nativity scenes, and markets filling the streets. It's also the perfect opportunity to indulge in hearty Neapolitan cuisine, which feels even more comforting during cooler weather.

Overall, spring and autumn are the most pleasant seasons for a balanced and enjoyable visit to Naples, while summer and winter offer unique experiences for those looking to explore the city during its livelier or quieter moments. Whichever season you choose, Naples promises an unforgettable experience full of history, culture, and stunning natural beauty.

ENTRY REQUIREMENTS AND VISAS

The best times to visit Naples are during the spring (April to June) and autumn (September to October) when the weather is mild, the crowds are manageable, and the city's charm is at its peak. During these months, Naples offers ideal conditions for sightseeing, outdoor adventures, and enjoying its rich cultural and culinary offerings.

Spring in Naples brings pleasant temperatures, typically ranging between 15°C (59°F) and 25°C (77°F), with blooming flowers and clear skies. It's a perfect time to explore the city's landmarks, such as the historic center, Pompeii, and Mount Vesuvius, without the intense summer heat. Cafés spill out onto the streets, markets buzz with local life, and coastal areas like the Amalfi Coast and the island of Capri are particularly beautiful during this season.

Autumn offers similarly comfortable weather, with temperatures ranging from 18°C (64°F) to 26°C (79°F) and fewer tourists compared to the summer months. The air is crisp and clear, making it a great time for hiking Vesuvius, visiting archaeological sites, or taking day trips along the coast. Autumn is also harvest season in the surrounding Campania region, which means an abundance of fresh produce, local festivals, and a chance to enjoy the region's wines and cuisine at their best.

Summer (July and August) is the busiest and hottest time of year in Naples, with temperatures often exceeding 30°C (86°F). While the city can feel crowded, especially around major tourist sites, summer is an excellent time for coastal trips, enjoying Naples' beaches, and exploring the nearby islands of Capri, Ischia, and Procida. If visiting in summer, it's best to plan activities in the early morning or evening to avoid the midday heat. This season also sees a lively calendar of festivals, open-air concerts, and events, adding a vibrant atmosphere to the city.

Winter (November to March) is the quietest time to visit Naples, with fewer crowds and cooler temperatures ranging between 8°C (46°F) and 15°C (59°F). While some coastal areas may be less active, the city itself remains lively and full of charm. Winter is a great time to explore museums, churches, and archaeological sites at a relaxed pace. Naples is particularly beautiful during the Christmas season, with festive lights, elaborate nativity scenes, and markets filling the streets. It's also the perfect opportunity to indulge in hearty Neapolitan cuisine, which feels even more comforting during cooler weather.

Overall, spring and autumn are the most pleasant seasons for a balanced and enjoyable visit to Naples, while summer and winter offer unique experiences for those looking to explore the city during its livelier or quieter moments. Whichever season you choose, Naples promises an unforgettable experience full of history, culture, and stunning natural beauty.

GETTING TO NAPLES

Getting to Naples is convenient, as the city is well connected to both domestic and international destinations by air, rail, road, and sea. Whether you're flying in, arriving by train, driving, or traveling by ferry, Naples offers excellent transportation options to suit every traveler's needs.

Naples is served by Naples International Airport (Aeroporto di Napoli-Capodichino, NAP), located just 7 kilometers (4 miles) northeast of the city center. The airport provides direct flights to major European cities such as London, Paris, Madrid, and Frankfurt, along with domestic routes connecting Naples to cities like Rome, Milan, and Venice. Upon arrival, travelers have several options for reaching the city center. The Alibus shuttle service is a convenient choice, running regularly between the airport, Naples Central Station (Stazione Napoli Centrale), and the Port of Naples, with a journey time of approximately 15-30 minutes. Taxis are available outside the terminal with fixed fares to the city center, although it's important to confirm the fare before departing. For those seeking comfort or traveling with luggage, private transfers and car rental services are also available directly at the airport.

For travelers arriving by train, Naples is a major railway hub in southern Italy and benefits from excellent connections via Italy's high-speed train network. Naples Central Station (Stazione Napoli Centrale), located in Piazza Garibaldi, is the city's primary rail terminal. High-speed services such as Trenitalia's Frecciarossa and Italo connect Naples to major Italian cities quickly and efficiently, with travel times as short as 1 hour 10 minutes from Rome, 2 hours 30 minutes from Florence, and 4 hours 30 minutes from Milan. Regional trains also link Naples to nearby destinations like Sorrento, Salerno, and Caserta. The Circumvesuviana train line is particularly popular for reaching iconic sites like Pompeii, Herculaneum, and the Sorrentine Peninsula. Once at the station, Naples' metro system, buses, and taxis provide easy transfers to other parts of the city, ensuring seamless onward travel.

Travelers driving to Naples will find the city easily accessible via Italy's highway network, particularly the A1 Autostrada del Sole, which connects Naples to Rome and northern Italy. Driving offers flexibility, especially for visitors planning to explore nearby attractions such as the Amalfi Coast, Mount Vesuvius, and the islands of Capri and Ischia. However, driving within Naples can be challenging due to narrow streets, traffic congestion, and limited parking options. For a smoother experience, visitors can park in secure garages or designated lots near the city center and use public transportation or taxis to get around Naples.

For those arriving by sea, Naples' Port of Naples (Porto di Napoli) is one of the busiest and most important ports in the Mediterranean. It serves ferries, hydrofoils, and cruise ships, welcoming passengers from both domestic and international routes. Ferries connect Naples to nearby islands such as Capri, Ischia, and Procida, as well as coastal destinations like Sorrento and the Amalfi Coast. For fast connections to the islands, travelers can use the Beverello Pier, which serves as the main terminal for passenger ferries and hydrofoils. Additionally, the port accommodates cruise ships, making Naples a key stop for Mediterranean cruises arriving from cities like Palermo, Cagliari, and international ports.

Long-distance buses also provide a budget-friendly option for reaching Naples, connecting the city to other Italian and European destinations. Buses typically arrive at Napoli Centrale Station or the adjacent Metropark Terminal, offering easy access to the rest of the city. Companies like FlixBus and MarinoBus operate comfortable and affordable routes, making them a good alternative for travelers seeking cost-effective options.

Once you've arrived in Naples, the city is easy to navigate with its efficient public transportation system. Metro lines, buses, trams, and funiculars connect all the major neighborhoods, while taxis and rideshare options are widely available. For those who enjoy exploring on foot, the historic center is compact and best experienced by walking, as it allows you to immerse yourself in the vibrant atmosphere, discover hidden alleys, and appreciate the authentic charm of Naples.

No matter how you choose to travel, Naples is well prepared to welcome visitors with its wide range of transportation options, ensuring a smooth start to your journey through this captivating and historic city. Whether arriving by air, rail, road, or sea, the experience of stepping into Naples marks the beginning of an unforgettable adventure.

TRANSPORTATION

Naples offers a wide variety of transportation options that make it easy to navigate the city and explore its surroundings. From an efficient public transportation network to taxis, walking routes, and ferry connections, getting around Naples is both convenient and accessible for visitors.

The Naples Metro is one of the fastest and most efficient ways to travel across the city. The metro system consists of three main lines, with Line 1 (the Metro dell'Arte) being particularly notable for its beautifully designed stations, such as Toledo and Università, which are works of art in themselves. Line 1 connects key areas like the central station (Garibaldi) to the historic center, Vomero, and other popular neighborhoods. Line 2 is ideal for longer journeys, linking Naples' central station with districts further afield and offering connections to suburban areas.

In addition to the metro, Naples has a network of buses and trams that provide extensive coverage throughout the city. While buses are a convenient option for reaching areas not served by the metro, they can be affected by traffic congestion during peak hours. The main bus hub is located at Piazza Garibaldi, near Naples Central Station, where travelers can find routes to various neighborhoods and tourist sites. Tickets for buses, trams, and the metro can be purchased at newsstands, tobacconists (tabacchi), or vending machines at major stops. A single ticket is valid for 90 minutes across all forms of public transport within the city, while daily or weekly passes offer better value for longer stays.

For traveling up Naples' hilly areas, the funicular railways are both practical and scenic. Naples has four funicular lines—Central, Chiaia, Montesanto, and Mergellina—which connect the city's lower areas with higher districts like Vomero. These funiculars are especially useful for accessing panoramic viewpoints, attractions, and charming residential areas while avoiding steep climbs.

Walking is one of the best ways to experience Naples' vibrant atmosphere, particularly in the historic center. The narrow streets, bustling piazzas, and hidden corners of neighborhoods like Spaccanapoli and the Quartieri Spagnoli are best explored on foot, allowing you to fully immerse yourself in the city's energy, architecture, and culture. While walking, it's important to remain aware of traffic, as scooters and cars often navigate even the narrowest streets.

For visitors seeking more flexibility, taxis and rideshare services such as Uber are widely available throughout Naples. Taxis are a good option for short distances, particularly when public transportation is less accessible. However, it's recommended to use official taxis, which can be identified by their white color and official "TAXI" signs. Fares are metered, but it's always a good idea to confirm the approximate cost of your journey with the driver before departing.

Taxis can be hailed at taxi stands located in key areas like train stations, piazzas, and the airport.

To explore Naples' nearby islands and coastal destinations, the city's ferry and hydrofoil services provide excellent connections. From the Port of Naples (Porto di Napoli), travelers can catch ferries and fast hydrofoils to islands like Capri, Ischia, and Procida, as well as towns along the Amalfi Coast and Sorrento. The Beverello Pier is the main terminal for passenger ferries, while the Calata Porta di Massa terminal serves slower, larger ferries that are ideal for those traveling with cars. Hydrofoils offer faster journeys, making day trips to the islands both convenient and enjoyable.

For regional travel, Naples is well connected by trains, including the popular Circumvesuviana railway, which connects Naples to Pompeii, Herculaneum, Sorrento, and other towns along the Gulf of Naples. The Circumvesuviana trains depart from Naples Garibaldi Station, located below Naples Central Station, and provide affordable and reliable transportation for travelers exploring these famous sites. In addition, regional and high-speed trains from Trenitalia and Italo connect Naples to other major Italian cities and regions, making it an ideal base for broader travel throughout Italy.

Naples also has a bike-sharing system for visitors who enjoy cycling, although navigating the city by bike can be challenging due to uneven streets and busy traffic. For a more relaxed experience, cycling along the waterfront promenade, Lungomare Caracciolo, offers stunning views of the sea and Mount Vesuvius.

Whether you prefer the speed and convenience of the metro, the scenic funicular rides, the flexibility of taxis, or exploring on foot, Naples offers a diverse range of transportation options to suit all travel styles. Navigating the city and its surroundings is simple, allowing visitors to discover its landmarks, neighborhoods, and coastal beauty with ease.

CHAPTER TWO

GETTING AROUND NAPLES

PUBLIC TRANSPORT

Public transport in Naples is efficient, affordable, and provides easy access to the city's key neighborhoods, landmarks, and surrounding areas. The system includes metro lines, buses, trams, funiculars, and regional trains, offering travelers multiple ways to get around the city and beyond.

The Naples Metro is one of the most popular modes of public transport, with its modern and reliable services. The metro system has three main lines, with Line 1 (also known as the Metro dell'Arte) being particularly renowned for its beautifully designed art stations. Stations like Toledo, considered one of the most stunning metro stations in Europe, and Università, with its sleek and artistic interiors, turn a simple commute into a visual experience. Line 1 connects the central station at Garibaldi to key areas such as the historic center, Vomero, and several cultural attractions. Line 2 runs from Pozzuoli through the central station and connects to the city's outskirts, making it ideal for longer journeys. Line 6, though limited, links parts of the coastal area.

Naples also has an extensive bus and tram network that covers the entire city, providing access to neighborhoods not served by the metro. The buses are operated by ANM (Azienda Napoletana Mobilità), and while they are affordable and connect most of Naples, traffic congestion during peak hours can sometimes cause delays. Trams are another option for reaching parts of the city center and surrounding areas, offering a scenic way to travel along select routes. The main bus hub is located at Piazza Garibaldi near Naples Central Station, where travelers can find routes leading to various neighborhoods and popular sights. Tickets for buses, trams, and metro services are integrated, allowing for seamless transfers within the network.

For those heading to Naples' hilly districts, the funicular railways are a practical and scenic option. The city has four funicular lines—Centrale, Chiaia, Montesanto, and Mergellina—that connect the lower parts of Naples to the upper areas, such as Vomero and Posillipo. These funiculars are particularly useful for avoiding steep climbs and provide stunning views of the city and the Bay of Naples during the short rides. The Centrale Funicular, in particular, links the central area near Via Toledo to the Vomero district, where visitors can explore landmarks like Castel Sant'Elmo and the Certosa di San Martino.

Public transportation also connects Naples to nearby attractions and destinations. The

Circumvesuviana railway, a regional train line, is essential for travelers planning day trips to Pompeii, Herculaneum, and Sorrento. Departing from Naples Garibaldi Station, these trains are affordable and reliable, providing a direct route to some of the region's most famous archaeological and coastal sites. Other regional train services, operated by Trenitalia, link Naples to surrounding towns, while EAV Campania offers additional local connections.

Tickets for all forms of public transport in Naples can be purchased at metro stations, bus stops, newsstands, and tobacconists (marked with a T sign). A standard ticket, called the UNICO ticket, is valid for 90 minutes across metro, buses, and trams, while daily, weekly, and monthly passes offer cost-effective options for longer stays or frequent use. To avoid fines, travelers must validate their tickets upon boarding buses and trams or before entering metro platforms.

Public transport in Naples is reliable and well integrated, making it easy for visitors to explore the city's highlights, including its historic center, bustling neighborhoods, and panoramic viewpoints. Whether traveling underground on the metro, climbing hills on a funicular, or enjoying scenic bus routes, Naples' public transport system offers an affordable and practical way to discover the vibrant and dynamic city.

WALKING AND EXPLORING NEIGHBOURHOODS

Walking is one of the best ways to explore Naples, allowing visitors to fully immerse themselves in the city's vibrant atmosphere, historic charm, and local life. Naples' neighborhoods are a patchwork of diverse areas, each with its own character, energy, and stories to tell. Exploring on foot reveals hidden alleys, architectural gems, colorful markets, and the authentic spirit of this ancient yet lively city.

The historic center (Centro Storico) is the heart of Naples and a UNESCO World Heritage Site, making it an essential starting point for walking tours. This area is a labyrinth of narrow, cobbled streets, bustling piazzas, and ornate churches, where every corner offers a glimpse of the city's rich history. Key streets like Spaccanapoli and Via dei Tribunali are ideal walking routes, as they cut through the historic center and lead to iconic sites such as the Church of Gesù Nuovo, the Sansevero Chapel, and the Naples Cathedral (Duomo di San Gennaro). Along the way, visitors can stop at small family-run shops, sample local treats like sfogliatella and pizza margherita, and observe Neapolitans going about their daily routines.

Walking through the Quartieri Spagnoli, located just off Via Toledo, offers a more raw and authentic experience. This bustling neighborhood is famous for its maze of narrow streets, colorful laundry hanging from balconies, and vibrant street life. Here, visitors can discover hidden churches, local trattorias, and artisan workshops, capturing the true essence of Naples. The Quartieri Spagnoli is also home to stunning street art, including murals and portraits that celebrate the city's culture and icons. Walking through this area gives a sense of Naples' layered identity—gritty, lively, and full of character.

For a more elegant and relaxed atmosphere, the Chiaia district is perfect for leisurely strolls. This upscale neighborhood, located along the seafront, features charming streets lined with boutique shops, art galleries, and stylish cafés. The Lungomare Caracciolo, Naples' scenic waterfront promenade, is a highlight of the area and offers stunning views of the Bay of Naples, Mount Vesuvius, and Castel dell'Ovo. Walking along the Lungomare is particularly enjoyable at sunset, when the light softens over the water, creating a magical atmosphere.

The Vomero district, perched on the hills overlooking Naples, combines panoramic views with a relaxed neighborhood vibe. Visitors can take one of the city's funiculars up to Vomero and explore its wide, tree-lined streets and elegant piazzas. Highlights include Castel Sant'Elmo, a 14th-century fortress that offers breathtaking 360-degree views of the city, and the nearby Certosa di San Martino, a former monastery with beautiful architecture and an extensive art collection. Vomero's open spaces and scenic outlooks make it a refreshing contrast to the dense streets of the historic center.

Another neighborhood worth exploring on foot is the vibrant Mercato and Porto district, where visitors can experience Naples' maritime roots. This area includes the bustling Piazza del Mercato and the Port of Naples, where ferries connect the city to nearby islands like Capri, Ischia, and Procida. Walking here offers a glimpse into Naples' commercial history, with fish markets, street vendors, and portside activity painting a vivid picture of local life.

For art and culture lovers, a walk through Rione Sanità is an unforgettable experience. Once considered off the beaten path, this historic neighborhood is now a vibrant area filled with artistic energy and cultural sites. The Catacombs of San Gennaro and Catacombs of San Gaudioso are highlights, offering a unique underground exploration of Naples' early Christian history. Above ground, the neighborhood's colorful palaces, street art, and local markets showcase its dynamic and evolving identity.

Walking in Naples also offers the opportunity to discover its piazzas, which serve as lively gathering places for locals and visitors alike. The elegant Piazza del Plebiscito, the city's largest square, is an ideal spot for people-watching and admiring architectural landmarks like the Royal Palace and the Basilica of San Francesco di Paola. Smaller squares like Piazza Bellini and Piazza San Domenico Maggiore are equally charming, often bustling with students, musicians, and outdoor cafés.

While exploring Naples on foot is a rewarding experience, it's important to remain aware of the city's unique rhythm. The streets are often busy with scooters, cars, and pedestrians sharing narrow spaces, so staying alert is essential, especially when crossing streets or navigating crowded areas. Wearing comfortable shoes is highly recommended, as the cobblestone streets and hills can be challenging for long walks.

Walking through Naples allows visitors to connect with the city's soul, uncover its layered history, and experience its unmatched energy. Whether wandering through ancient streets, climbing hills for panoramic views, or strolling along the waterfront, exploring Naples on foot is the best way to discover its beauty, character, and vibrant local life.

CAR RENTALS AND DRIVING TIPS

Renting a car in Naples can be a practical option for travelers who wish to explore the surrounding areas, such as the Amalfi Coast, Pompeii, Sorrento, and the beautiful countryside of Campania. While Naples itself can be challenging to drive in due to heavy traffic, narrow streets, and bold driving habits, having a car offers flexibility and convenience for visiting destinations beyond the city.

Car rental services are widely available throughout Naples, with major international providers like Hertz, Avis, Europcar, Sixt, and Enterprise, as well as local agencies, offering a variety of vehicles. Rental offices can be found at

Naples International Airport (Capodichino), Naples Central Station (Stazione Napoli Centrale), and in various locations across the city center. Booking your rental car in advance is recommended, especially during high tourist seasons, such as summer, when availability becomes limited.

Most car rental agencies require drivers to be at least 21 years old, although some companies may charge an additional fee for drivers under 25. A valid driver's license is required, and international visitors are often advised to carry an International Driving Permit (IDP) alongside their domestic license. Additionally, a credit card is typically needed to secure the rental deposit, and renters should consider purchasing comprehensive insurance coverage for theft, damage, and liability to ensure peace of mind.

Driving in Naples is not for the faint of heart and may present challenges for visitors unfamiliar with the city's traffic. The local driving style is bold, spontaneous, and often involves heavy use of horns for communication rather than aggression. Streets in Naples, particularly in the historic center and neighborhoods like the Quartieri Spagnoli, are narrow and congested, requiring careful maneuvering. Traffic congestion is frequent, especially during rush hours, so patience and alertness are essential when navigating city roads.

When driving, visitors should be mindful of ZTL zones (Zona a Traffico Limitato)—restricted traffic areas enforced in parts of Naples, particularly in the historic center. These zones are monitored by cameras, and unauthorized vehicles entering a ZTL can incur substantial fines. It is important to familiarize yourself with ZTL boundaries, which are often marked with clear signage, and discuss them with your car rental provider to avoid unexpected penalties.

Parking in Naples can be another challenge due to limited spaces and strict parking enforcement. Visitors should look for secure parking garages or designated parking areas to avoid fines or towing. Public parking spaces are marked with different colored lines:

1. Blue lines indicate paid parking zones, where tickets can be purchased from machines, tobacconists (tabacchi), or mobile apps.
2. White lines denote free parking spaces, though these are rare and often in high demand.
3. Yellow lines are reserved for residents, official vehicles, or specific uses and should be avoided.

Using private parking garages is often the best option, as they offer secure and convenient parking at reasonable rates. Visitors may also consider parking their vehicles on the outskirts of Naples and using public transportation, taxis, or walking to explore the busy city center.

While driving in Naples itself can be intense, renting a car becomes an invaluable advantage when venturing beyond the city to explore the stunning Campania region. One of the most popular road trips is the drive along the Amalfi Coast, which is famed for its dramatic cliffs, scenic coastal views, and picturesque towns like Positano, Ravello, and Amalfi. However, this route features winding, narrow roads with sharp curves and can be crowded during peak travel months, so confident and cautious driving is essential.

For visitors interested in history, a car rental allows for convenient day trips to ancient sites such as Pompeii and Herculaneum, which are located near Mount Vesuvius. Both sites are easily accessible by car and offer a fascinating glimpse into life during the Roman Empire. Driving to nearby towns like Sorrento and Caserta, home to the magnificent Royal Palace of

Caserta, is also straightforward and offers flexibility to explore these areas at your own pace.

Travelers planning to visit Naples' islands, such as Capri, Ischia, and Procida, should note that cars are generally not necessary on the islands. It is best to park at the Port of Naples and take a ferry to the islands, where walking or public transportation is sufficient for getting around.

To ensure a smooth driving experience, it is important to remain patient, alert, and mindful of local habits. Always yield to pedestrians, particularly in busy areas, and keep an eye out for scooters, which are a common and sometimes unpredictable presence on Naples' roads. Driving outside the city, however, is far less stressful, with open roads and scenic routes offering a much calmer experience.

Renting a car in Naples gives visitors the freedom to explore the surrounding region's natural beauty, historic landmarks, and charming towns at their own pace. While navigating Naples requires extra care and confidence, the rewards of discovering hidden gems and breathtaking landscapes beyond the city make it a worthwhile choice for travelers.

CHAPTER THREE

WHERE TO STAY

BEST NEIGHBOURHOODS FOR VISITORS

Naples is a city of contrasts, with each neighborhood offering its own unique character, atmosphere, and set of attractions. Whether you're seeking rich history, vibrant street life, stunning views, or trendy dining spots, Naples has a neighborhood to suit every type of visitor. Here are some of the best neighborhoods for travelers to explore:

- Centro Storico (Historic Center)

The historic heart of Naples, and a UNESCO World Heritage Site, is one of the most fascinating areas to explore. The Centro Storico is a maze of narrow streets, vibrant piazzas, and stunning architectural landmarks. Here, visitors can walk through the heart of Neapolitan culture, discovering sites like the Naples Cathedral (Duomo di San Gennaro), the Church of Gesù Nuovo, and the Sansevero Chapel, home to the famous Veiled Christ sculpture. The area is also known for its lively street markets, artisan shops, and traditional trattorias serving authentic Neapolitan pizza. Spaccanapoli is one of the most famous streets here, cutting through the heart of the district and offering a snapshot of local life.

- Quartieri Spagnoli (Spanish Quarter)

For an authentic, off-the-beaten-path experience, the Quartieri Spagnoli offers a taste of true Neapolitan life. This dense and vibrant neighborhood is filled with narrow alleys, colorful buildings, and bustling local markets. It's the perfect place to witness everyday life in Naples, with laundry hanging out of windows, street vendors selling fresh produce, and small family-owned shops. The area is full of traditional pizzerias and hidden gems, making it ideal for those looking to immerse themselves in Naples' local culture. Though slightly chaotic, the Quartieri Spagnoli offers a real, unpolished experience of the city, with stunning views of the Bay of Naples and Castel Sant'Elmo from the higher streets.

- Vomero

Located on the hills above the city center, Vomero is one of the most scenic neighborhoods in Naples. Known for its panoramic views, this upscale area offers a more relaxed atmosphere compared to the hustle and bustle of the city center. Vomero is home to charming piazzas, beautiful villas, and parks, making it an ideal spot for leisurely strolls. Castel Sant'Elmo and the nearby Certosa di San Martino offer stunning views of Naples, Mount Vesuvius, and the Bay of Naples. Vomero also has some of the city's best shopping and dining options, as well as a lively café culture. The neighborhood is easily accessible via the funicular, which takes visitors from the city center up the hill.

- Chiaia

For a more sophisticated and tranquil experience, Chiaia offers a beautiful mix of upscale shops, elegant buildings, and beautiful sea views. This neighborhood is perfect for those looking to experience the more refined side of Naples, with its stylish boutiques, art galleries, and chic cafes. The area is also home to the stunning Lungomare Caracciolo, a scenic seafront promenade that offers breathtaking views of the Bay of Naples and Mount Vesuvius. Piazza dei Martiri is the heart of Chiaia, where visitors can find designer stores and enjoy a leisurely coffee. Chiaia is also well known for its nightlife, with a range of sophisticated bars and restaurants along the waterfront.

- Rione Sanità

Rione Sanità is an increasingly vibrant area that is rich in history, art, and culture. Historically a working-class district, it has undergone a transformation in recent years, becoming a hub for local artists, performers, and creative projects. Visitors to Rione Sanità can explore its fascinating catacombs, such as the Catacombs of San Gennaro and Catacombs of San Gaudioso, which offer a glimpse into the city's early Christian past. The neighborhood also boasts stunning Baroque architecture, colorful street art, and unique cultural venues. Rione Sanità is a great place to explore on foot, discovering hidden gems and experiencing Naples' local culture.

- Piazza del Plebiscito & Royal Palace Area

For visitors who want to see the grandeur of Naples, the area around Piazza del Plebiscito is a must-visit. This grand square is flanked by two iconic buildings: the Royal Palace of Naples and the Basilica of San Francesco di Paola. The area is one of the most beautiful in the city, with elegant architecture, spacious piazzas, and a refined atmosphere. From here, visitors can easily access Teatro di San Carlo, one of the oldest and most famous opera houses in Europe. The Galleria Umberto I, a stunning shopping arcade with glass ceilings, is also located nearby. This central area is great for a leisurely walk, visiting historic landmarks, and enjoying the city's more elegant side.

- Mercato & Porto

The Mercato district, located near the Port of Naples, is one of the city's most vibrant and dynamic areas. This bustling neighborhood is full of energy, with street vendors selling fresh produce, fish markets, and lively squares. The Porto area, with its maritime connections, offers a glimpse into Naples' seafaring history and is the gateway to the islands of Capri, Ischia, and Procida. The Piazza del Mercato is the main square, home to historical sites and busy market stalls. It's a great neighborhood for those interested in Naples' maritime culture, with easy access to the waterfront and the ferries that connect the city to the nearby islands.

- Porto di Mergellina & Posillipo

For visitors looking for a more peaceful, residential area with incredible sea views, Mergellina and Posillipo offer a tranquil retreat from the city's busy streets. These neighborhoods are located along the coast, offering stunning views of the Bay of Naples, Mount Vesuvius, and the surrounding hills. The Lungomare di Mergellina is a beautiful promenade where you can walk along the water, enjoy a meal at one of the waterfront restaurants, and watch the boats sail by. Posillipo is a more upscale area, known for its luxurious villas, gardens, and panoramic vistas. It's a great place for visitors who want to escape the crowds while still being close to the city's main attractions.

Each neighborhood in Naples has its own distinct vibe, from the historic and bustling streets of the Centro Storico to the serene and scenic beauty of Vomero and Posillipo. Whether you're looking for a deep dive into history, a taste of local life, or a peaceful escape with breathtaking views, Naples' neighborhoods offer a diverse range of experiences for every type of traveler.

LUXURY HOTELS AND RESORTS

Naples offers a range of luxurious accommodations for travelers seeking the ultimate in comfort, service, and elegance. From opulent hotels with historic charm to modern resorts overlooking the stunning Bay of Naples, these properties provide exceptional amenities, prime locations, and unforgettable views. Here are some of the best luxury hotels and resorts in the city and surrounding areas.

The Grand Hotel Vesuvio is one of Naples' most iconic luxury hotels, offering a blend of classic elegance and modern luxury. Located along the seafront, the hotel boasts breathtaking views of the Bay of Naples, Mount Vesuvius, and Castel dell'Ovo. The spacious rooms and suites are decorated in a traditional style, with many featuring private balconies overlooking the sea. The hotel's rooftop restaurant, La Terrazza, serves Mediterranean cuisine with stunning views, making it a favorite for high-end travelers. Its central location adds to its appeal, offering easy access to key attractions.

For those seeking a more contemporary experience, Romeo Hotel is a stylish, modern hotel near the waterfront. This five-star property combines cutting-edge design with top-tier facilities, including a luxurious spa, rooftop pool, and several gourmet restaurants. The rooms and suites are sleek and spacious, with panoramic views of the Gulf of Naples. The hotel's

Michelin-starred restaurant, Il Comandante, offers fine dining with a view. Its proximity to the Port of Naples makes it a convenient base for those traveling to nearby islands.

Palazzo Caracciolo Napoli – MGallery Collection is a former aristocratic palace turned five-star hotel, offering a perfect blend of historic architecture and modern luxury. Located in the heart of the city, this hotel offers unique accommodations combining classical Neapolitan elements with contemporary design. The property features charming courtyards, a private garden, and a relaxing spa. Guests are within walking distance of Piazza del Plebiscito, the Royal Palace, and other historic landmarks, making it a central and elegant place to stay.

Excelsior Hotel, located near the Lungomare Caracciolo with views of the bay and Mount Vesuvius, is one of Naples' most prestigious hotels. Combining old-world charm with modern luxury, this grand hotel offers spacious rooms and suites, many with panoramic views. The rooftop restaurant provides spectacular views, and guests can enjoy fine dining while overlooking the bay. Its prime location makes it an excellent choice for those seeking both luxury and convenience, with easy access to shopping, dining, and cultural sites.

Hotel San Francesco al Monte is set in a historic 16th-century monastery in the Vomero district, offering a unique luxury experience with a strong sense of history. The hotel offers stunning views of Naples, Mount Vesuvius, and the Bay of Naples. Guests can enjoy spacious, elegantly decorated rooms, many with private terraces. The hotel features a rooftop garden, a gourmet restaurant, and an outdoor pool, making it a perfect spot for relaxation. The peaceful setting, combined with its proximity to the historic center, provides a charming and refined place to stay.

Le Sirenuse, while not directly in Naples, is a short drive away in Positano, one of the most luxurious resorts on the Amalfi Coast. Perched above the colorful town, the hotel offers stunning views of the Mediterranean Sea and the cliffs of Positano. Known for its impeccable service and exceptional beauty, Le Sirenuse offers Mediterranean-inspired rooms, many with private terraces. The hotel features a Michelin-starred restaurant, a world-class spa, and an outdoor pool with sweeping views, making it an ideal retreat for those seeking serenity and luxury on the Amalfi Coast.

The Blue Bay Hotel, located in the quieter Posillipo district, offers sophisticated accommodations with breathtaking views of the Gulf of Naples. Known for its modern design and elegant interiors, the hotel combines spacious rooms, suites, and private villas, many with sea views. The exclusive beachfront location, wellness center, and gourmet restaurant ensure a relaxing and upscale experience, with easy access to both Naples and the surrounding coastal beauty.

MID-RANGE AND BOUTIQUE ACCOMMODATIONS

Naples offers a wide range of mid-range and boutique accommodations that combine comfort, style, and affordability. These hotels and guesthouses offer a more intimate, personalized experience, often with unique décor, central locations, and a cozy atmosphere, making them an excellent choice for travelers who want to experience the charm of the city without the high-end price tag.

- Hotel Piazza Bellini

Located in the heart of Naples, Hotel Piazza Bellini offers a charming boutique experience in the city's historic center. The hotel is housed in a 16th-century building and features a mix of contemporary design and classic Neapolitan architecture. Guests can enjoy spacious rooms, some of which have private balconies overlooking the bustling square. The hotel's location is ideal for exploring Naples' main attractions, including the Museo Archeologico Nazionale and Spaccanapoli. The vibrant courtyard and bar area provide a relaxing place to unwind after a day of sightseeing.

- Naples Grande Hotel

Situated near the Lungomare with stunning views of the Gulf of Naples, Naples Grande Hotel offers a stylish and affordable stay. The rooms are modern and well-equipped, with many offering sea views. The hotel features an elegant rooftop bar, a fitness center, and a seasonal outdoor pool, making it a great choice for those seeking both relaxation and convenience. Its location offers easy access to the city's historic center and is perfect for visitors wanting to be close to both cultural landmarks and the sea.

- Hotel Art Resort Galleria Umberto

Nestled within the famous Galleria Umberto I, Hotel Art Resort offers a boutique experience with an artistic flair. The hotel is decorated with contemporary art, offering a creative and inspiring atmosphere. The rooms are stylish and comfortable, with modern amenities and elegant furnishings. The hotel's location, within walking distance of Teatro di San Carlo and Piazza del Plebiscito, makes it ideal for those wanting to experience Naples' cultural offerings. Guests can also enjoy the vibrant café scene and chic shops of the Galleria Umberto right on their doorstep.

- Chiaja Hotel de Charme

For a more intimate and classic Italian experience, Chiaja Hotel de Charme offers a cozy, boutique stay in the Chiaia district. The hotel is housed in a charming historical building and features elegant, well-appointed rooms with a mix of traditional and modern elements. Located just a short walk from the Lungomare and Piazza del

Plebiscito, this hotel provides a perfect base for exploring Naples. The property's friendly service and attention to detail make it a popular choice for visitors seeking a personalized experience.

- La Ciliegina Lifestyle Hotel

Located near the Piazza Municipio, La Ciliegina Lifestyle Hotel is a modern, boutique hotel offering a comfortable and stylish stay. The hotel features contemporary rooms with sleek design and high-end amenities, including a rooftop terrace with views of the city and the Bay of Naples. It's an ideal option for travelers looking for a more relaxed atmosphere without compromising on style or convenience. The hotel's central location makes it easy to explore nearby attractions, such as Castel Nuovo and the Naples National Archaeological Museum.

- Hotel Il Convento

Located in the Spaccanapoli area, Hotel Il Convento offers a charming and affordable stay in the heart of the historic center. The hotel is set in a former convent, combining traditional architectural elements with modern touches. The rooms are warm and welcoming, offering a cozy ambiance with classic furnishings. The location is perfect for those wanting to explore Naples on foot, with the Duomo di San Gennaro, San Gregorio Armeno, and other famous landmarks just a short walk away. The hotel's intimate size and welcoming staff make it a favorite among visitors.

- B&B Palazzo San Vincenzo

For a more intimate and home-like experience, B&B Palazzo San Vincenzo offers a charming stay in the historic center of Naples. Set in a 17th-century building, this bed and breakfast combines old-world charm with modern amenities. The rooms are comfortable, featuring classic décor, and some come with views of the Castel Nuovo or the Bay of Naples. The B&B is located near key attractions like Piazza del

Plebiscito and Teatro di San Carlo, providing a convenient base for exploring the city. Guests appreciate the personalized service and homely atmosphere, making it a great option for those looking for a more personal touch.

- Relais sul Mare

Set in the scenic Mergellina district, Relais sul Mare offers stunning views of the Gulf of Naples and Mount Vesuvius. This boutique guesthouse provides a more intimate and relaxed stay with modern amenities and personalized service. Rooms are elegantly decorated and come with sea-facing balconies. Guests can enjoy a hearty breakfast while overlooking the water, and the property is ideally located for those wishing to explore both the Lungomare and the vibrant Chiaia district. Its tranquil atmosphere makes it perfect for those wanting a quiet retreat near the city center.

- Hotel Portavalisa

In the heart of the Centro Storico, Hotel Portavalisa provides a unique blend of boutique luxury and history. Housed in a beautifully restored building, this hotel offers modern, comfortable rooms with a historical flair. Its central location puts guests just a short walk away from Naples' major landmarks, such as San Carlo Theatre and Spaccanapoli. The intimate, personal service makes it a great choice for those seeking a more relaxed, yet centrally located, experience in Naples.

These mid-range and boutique accommodations offer a personalized, comfortable, and affordable stay in Naples, making them perfect for travelers who want to enjoy the city's rich culture, history, and atmosphere while avoiding the luxury price tag. Whether you're staying in the heart of the historic center, near the seafront, or in quieter neighborhoods, these properties provide an excellent base for discovering the best of Naples.

BUDGET-FRIENDLY OPTIONS

Naples offers several budget-friendly options for travelers looking to experience the city without breaking the bank. From simple, comfortable hotels to cozy guesthouses and hostels, these accommodations provide good value, excellent locations, and a chance to experience the charm of Naples at a more affordable price. Here are some budget-friendly options in Naples:

- Hotel Juliet

Located in the heart of Naples, Hotel Juliet offers affordable rates with a central location. The rooms are simple yet comfortable, providing all the necessary amenities for a pleasant stay. The hotel is within walking distance of major attractions like Piazza del Plebiscito, the Royal Palace, and the Lungomare, making it an excellent base for exploring the city. The friendly staff and relaxed atmosphere add to the hotel's appeal for budget-conscious travelers.

- B&B La Dimora di Nettuno

For a cozy and affordable stay, B&B La Dimora di Nettuno offers a comfortable option near the city center. This charming bed and breakfast is set in a historic building and features basic yet well-maintained rooms. It's located near the Port of Naples, making it a great choice for those traveling to the nearby islands. Guests can enjoy a delicious breakfast and personalized service, which makes for a welcoming and budget-friendly experience.

- Hostel of the Sun

Hostel of the Sun is one of the most popular budget hostels in Naples, known for its friendly and welcoming atmosphere. Located near the Lungomare, the hostel offers dormitory-style rooms and private rooms at affordable rates. It's perfect for travelers who want to meet fellow backpackers and enjoy a lively, social atmosphere. The hostel also offers a fully equipped kitchen, free Wi-Fi, and helpful staff who can assist with tips and recommendations for exploring Naples. The central location allows easy access to public transport and major attractions.

- B&B Napoliamo

B&B Napoliamo is a great option for those seeking budget accommodations in the historic center of Naples. The rooms are simple but clean, with comfortable beds and basic amenities. The B&B is just a short walk from Spaccanapoli, San Gregorio Armeno, and the Naples Cathedral, so it's perfect for visitors wanting to explore the city on foot. The staff is friendly and eager to provide recommendations for local dining and sightseeing, adding to the homely feel of this budget-friendly option.

- Hotel Neapolis

Hotel Neapolis is a charming budget hotel located in the Centro Storico. With simple, comfortable rooms and a warm, welcoming atmosphere, this hotel offers great value for money. Guests can enjoy a convenient location near the National Archaeological Museum and Piazza del Gesù Nuovo, making it ideal for exploring the city's cultural heritage. The hotel provides free Wi-Fi and a breakfast service, making it a great budget choice for travelers seeking comfort and convenience.

- B&B Casa Tonia

For an affordable and cozy option, B&B Casa Tonia offers simple rooms with traditional Neapolitan décor in the Vomero district. It is a quiet, residential area that provides a relaxing atmosphere while still being easily accessible to the main attractions of the city. The rooms come with essential amenities and a hearty breakfast to start your day. The B&B is known for its hospitality, and the host goes out of their way to provide guests with helpful advice and local tips. The neighborhood also offers great views of the city and is a short distance from the Certosa di San Martino and Castel Sant'Elmo.

- La Casa di Toto

Located in the Quartieri Spagnoli, La Casa di Toto offers a more traditional and local experience at budget prices. The rooms are simple but clean, and the property's location in one of Naples' most authentic neighborhoods offers an immersive experience. The area is known for its vibrant street life, bustling markets, and local eateries, so you'll get a taste of Naples' culture right outside your door. This is an ideal choice for those looking to stay in the heart of the city and enjoy the atmosphere of the Spanish Quarter.

- Hotel Europeo & Flowers

Hotel Europeo & Flowers is a budget-friendly hotel located near Piazza Garibaldi and Naples Central Station, making it convenient for travelers arriving by train. The hotel offers basic rooms with essential amenities, including free Wi-Fi, and a comfortable stay at an affordable price. Its central location is perfect for those looking to explore the historic center, with easy access to public transport and popular sites like Spaccanapoli and Naples Cathedral.

- B&B L'Imbarcadero

Located in the Mergellina district, B&B L'Imbarcadero offers affordable rates with scenic views of the Gulf of Naples. The rooms are simple yet well-maintained, providing a comfortable and affordable base for your stay. The B&B is just a short walk from the Lungomare, where visitors can enjoy leisurely walks along the seafront or catch ferries to nearby islands. The location provides easy access to both the city center and the more peaceful coastal area.

- Affittacamere Pigna

This budget-friendly guesthouse offers simple and clean rooms in the heart of Naples, near Piazza del Plebiscito and the Royal Palace. Affittacamere Pigna offers excellent value for money, providing basic amenities like free Wi-Fi, air conditioning, and a central location for those looking to explore the historic center. The rooms are cozy and welcoming, and the staff provides great local recommendations, ensuring a pleasant stay without the high price tag.

These budget-friendly accommodations allow visitors to experience the best of Naples without spending a fortune. Whether you're looking for a simple hostel, a cozy bed and breakfast, or an affordable hotel, these options offer comfort, convenience, and excellent value. Each provides a great base for exploring Naples' vibrant neighborhoods, historical landmarks, and nearby attractions, all while sticking to a reasonable budget.

CHAPTER FOUR

TOP ATTRACTIONS AND LANDMARKS

THE HISTORIC CENTER OF NAPLES

The historic center of Naples, a UNESCO World Heritage Site, is one of the most fascinating and vibrant areas in the city, offering a rich tapestry of history, culture, and tradition. The district is a maze of narrow streets, charming piazzas, and centuries-old buildings, where the past and present seamlessly blend together. As the heart of the city, it is home to some of Naples' most iconic landmarks, churches, and museums, and offers visitors an authentic glimpse into the city's soul.

- Spaccanapoli

One of the most famous streets in the historic center, Spaccanapoli cuts through the heart of the old town and is lined with churches, shops, and local eateries. The street is vibrant and bustling, offering a sensory overload of sights, sounds, and smells, with street vendors selling everything from pizza to souvenirs. Along Spaccanapoli, visitors can discover some of the most important religious sites in Naples, including Santa Chiara, a beautiful Gothic church with a peaceful cloister, and San Domenico Maggiore, a church rich in history and artistic works.

- Piazza del Plebiscito

At the edge of the historic center lies Piazza del Plebiscito, one of the city's most impressive squares. Surrounded by grand architecture, including the Royal Palace of Naples and the Basilica of San Francesco di Paola, the square is a popular gathering place for both locals and visitors. The open space, with its vast stone pavements and views of the Gulf of Naples, provides a perfect spot to relax and take in the surroundings. The Royal Palace, once home to Spanish and later Bourbon kings, houses a museum that offers a glimpse into the royal history of Naples.

- Via San Gregorio Armeno

Known for its artisan shops and traditional Nativity scenes, Via San Gregorio Armeno is a picturesque street that is particularly popular during the Christmas season. The street is lined with small workshops where skilled artisans create intricate Presepi (Nativity scenes), which are sold as both religious decorations and pieces of art. The area is also home to the Church of San Gregorio Armeno, a Baroque masterpiece that adds to the street's historical and spiritual significance.

- Naples National Archaeological Museum

A must-see for history and archaeology lovers, the Naples National Archaeological Museum houses one of the most important collections of ancient Roman antiquities in the world. Located near the historic center, the museum contains a vast array of artifacts from the nearby ruins of Pompeii and Herculaneum, including mosaics, frescoes, sculptures, and everyday objects that offer a glimpse into daily life during the Roman Empire. The museum also features works of art from the ancient Greek and Egyptian worlds.

- The Duomo (Cathedral of Naples)

The Duomo di Napoli, also known as the Cathedral of Naples, is another important landmark in the historic center. This magnificent Gothic and Baroque cathedral is dedicated to Saint Januarius (San Gennaro), the patron saint of Naples. The cathedral is famous for housing the relics of San Gennaro, and it is a pilgrimage site for many. The cathedral's interior is adorned with stunning artworks and a beautiful frescoed dome, and visitors can also explore the crypt where San Gennaro's remains are kept.

- Via Toledo

A lively and bustling shopping street, Via Toledo stretches from Piazza Dante to the Gulf of Naples, offering a mix of high-end boutiques, department stores, and local shops. This vibrant street is a focal point for both locals and tourists, with its historical significance, as well as its role as a commercial hub. Via Toledo is also home to the Galleria Umberto I, a stunning glass-domed shopping gallery that is a great spot for a coffee break or some window shopping.

- Cappella Sansevero

A hidden gem in the historic center, Cappella Sansevero is a small, yet extraordinary, chapel that houses some of the most remarkable works of art in Naples. The Veiled Christ, a stunning marble sculpture by Giuseppe Sanmartino, is the centerpiece of the chapel. The intricate craftsmanship of this piece, which appears to show Christ with a veil made of marble, is a testament to the skill of the artist and the beauty of Baroque art. The chapel also features other sculptures and frescoes, making it a must-visit for art enthusiasts.

- Piazza Dante and the Pedamentina

At the western end of the historic center lies Piazza Dante, a lively square named after the Italian poet Dante Alighieri. The square is surrounded by cafes, restaurants, and historical buildings, and it provides access to the Pedamentina, a historic staircase that leads up to the Certosa di San Martino and Castel Sant'Elmo, both of which offer panoramic views of the city. The staircase is a picturesque route, offering visitors the chance to walk through beautiful neighborhoods while taking in the scenery.

- Underground Naples (Napoli Sotterranea)

For a different perspective on the historic center, visitors can explore Napoli Sotterranea, the underground tunnels beneath the city. This fascinating network of ancient Greek and Roman chambers, catacombs, and aqueducts offers a glimpse into the hidden history of Naples. Guided tours provide an informative look at the city's development, from its origins as a Greek colony to its growth during the Roman Empire.

- The Spanish Quarter (Quartieri Spagnoli)

The Spanish Quarter is one of the most authentic and lively neighborhoods in Naples. Located just off Spaccanapoli, the quarter is known for its narrow alleys, colorful buildings, and vibrant street life. It's a place where visitors can experience the true essence of Neapolitan life, with locals bustling through the streets, laundry hanging from balconies, and traditional shops offering everything from pizza to artisan goods. The Spanish Quarter is also home to several charming piazzas and historical sites, making it a great area for exploring on foot.

The historic center of Naples offers a unique and immersive experience, where visitors can wander through centuries of history, discover hidden treasures, and soak in the energy of one of Italy's most dynamic cities. From grand piazzas to narrow alleys, ancient churches to bustling markets, the center of Naples is a place where every corner tells a story. Whether you're exploring the rich cultural heritage, admiring the art and architecture, or enjoying the local food and atmosphere, the historic center is an unmissable part of any visit to the city.

NAPLES CATHEDRAL

Naples Cathedral (Cattedrale di Napoli), also known as the Cathedral of Saint Januarius (Duomo di San Gennaro), is one of the most important religious landmarks in the city. Located in the heart of the historic center, the cathedral is not only a center of religious worship but also a key piece of Naples' rich cultural and architectural heritage. It is dedicated to San Gennaro, the patron saint of Naples, and is renowned for its beautiful architecture, historic significance, and religious importance.

- Historical Significance

The cathedral was originally founded in the 13th century by Charles I of Anjou, although it was significantly renovated and expanded in later centuries, particularly during the Baroque period. The cathedral's history reflects the changing architectural styles and influences that have shaped Naples over the centuries. The church has been the site of several important events in the city's religious and political life, including the annual Feast of San Gennaro, when the saint's blood is said to liquefy in a miraculous event —a phenomenon that draws both devotion and curiosity.

- Architecture

The cathedral's exterior is an impressive mix of Gothic, Baroque, and Renaissance styles. The façade, built in the early 14th century, features intricate sculptures and elegant detailing, while the entrance is flanked by two large towers. The cathedral's interior is equally stunning, with a grand nave and multiple chapels dedicated to various saints. The most famous part of the interior is the Chapel of San Gennaro, which houses the saint's relics.

The Chapel of San Gennaro is a Baroque masterpiece, created in the 17th century. It is here that the faithful gather each year to witness the miracle of the blood of San Gennaro, an event that has been observed for centuries. The chapel features elaborate decorations, gilded altars, and ornate frescoes. The treasure of San Gennaro, a collection of precious relics and artifacts, is also housed in the cathedral and is a major draw for visitors.

- The Miracle of San Gennaro

One of the most unique and famous aspects of Naples Cathedral is the annual miracle of San

Gennaro's blood. The miracle occurs on September 19, the feast day of San Gennaro, and two other dates during the year. On these occasions, a vial of the saint's blood, kept in the cathedral, is said to liquefy, a phenomenon that is both a source of religious devotion and a topic of scientific intrigue. The event draws thousands of pilgrims, and the ritual is closely watched by the people of Naples, who believe it is a sign of the city's good fortune and divine protection.

- Art and Sculptures

In addition to the Chapel of San Gennaro, the cathedral houses several notable artworks, including frescoes, sculptures, and paintings. The frescoed ceiling, completed in the 16th century, depicts scenes from the life of San Gennaro. The Altar of the Virgin Mary, located in one of the side chapels, is another beautiful feature of the cathedral. The high altar of the cathedral is made of marble and features a stunning depiction of San Gennaro.

The cathedral also has several chapels, each with its own set of artworks. The Chapel of San Restituto, for example, contains remnants of an early Christian basilica that once stood on the same site. The Chapel of the Treasure of San Gennaro is particularly important as it is home to the saint's relics and the precious items associated with the miracle.

- Visiting Naples Cathedral

The cathedral is open to visitors year-round, and it remains an active place of worship, so visitors are encouraged to be respectful during services. There are guided tours available, which can help visitors better understand the cathedral's history, architecture, and the significance of San Gennaro. The Treasury Museum of San Gennaro is also a highlight for those interested in the relics and the history of the saint's miraculous blood.

The cathedral is located near other key landmarks in Naples, making it a convenient stop on a tour of the historic center. Its proximity to Spaccanapoli and Piazza del Plebiscito means it is easily accessible from other points of interest in the city.

Naples Cathedral is an essential stop for anyone interested in the history, art, and spirituality of Naples. Its magnificent architecture, the legendary miracle of San Gennaro, and its rich collection of art and relics make it a key part of the city's religious and cultural landscape. Whether visiting for the Feast of San Gennaro or simply exploring its historical beauty, Naples Cathedral offers a deep connection to the city's heritage and its enduring devotion to its patron saint.

CASTEL DELL'OVO AND CASTEL NUOVO

Castel dell'Ovo and Castel Nuovo are two of Naples' most iconic castles, each offering a distinct view of the city's rich history, architecture, and its role in shaping the region over centuries. Both castles are located near the seafront, allowing visitors to take in breathtaking views of the Gulf of Naples, while also providing a glimpse into the city's past as a center of power, defense, and culture.

- Castel dell'Ovo (Castle of the Egg)

Castel dell'Ovo is the oldest of Naples' major castles and sits along the seafront on Santa Lucia Hill. Its name, "Castle of the Egg," comes from a centuries-old legend that the Roman poet Virgil placed a magical egg in the castle's foundations to protect the city from misfortune. Originally built by the Romans as a fortress, Castel dell'Ovo was later expanded during the Norman and

Swabian periods, and its history reflects the various powers that ruled Naples. The castle has served as a military stronghold, a royal residence, and even a prison over the centuries. Its strategic location by the sea made it an essential defensive position for the city.

The architecture of Castel dell'Ovo is a blend of Roman, Medieval, and Renaissance styles, with its imposing walls and towers offering an imposing yet fascinating historical perspective. One of the key features of the castle is its bastions, which provide panoramic views of the Gulf of Naples, the city, and the imposing Mount Vesuvius. The Torre di Guardia (Guard Tower) is another prominent feature of the castle and offers stunning vistas of the surrounding area.

Today, Castel dell'Ovo is a museum and cultural venue, housing temporary art exhibitions and installations. It is free to visit, making it an accessible destination for tourists. Visitors can wander through the castle's open-air courtyards, enjoy the scenic views along the waterfront promenade, and learn about the castle's significant role in Naples' history.

- Castel Nuovo (Maschio Angioino)

Located near Piazza del Municipio, Castel Nuovo, also known as Maschio Angioino, is one of the most important landmarks in Naples. Built by the Angevins in 1279, the castle was initially intended to serve as a royal residence and a symbol of the power of the Angevin dynasty. Castel Nuovo has witnessed several pivotal moments in Naples' history, from the changes in rulers and dynasties to major sieges and battles that shaped the city's destiny.

The architecture of Castel Nuovo is a mix of Gothic and Renaissance styles, and it is one of the most impressive medieval fortresses in Italy. The castle's most striking feature is its Aragonese Arch, added during the Aragonese period in the 15th century. The arch is a masterpiece of Renaissance architecture and serves as the castle's main entrance, signifying the transition to a new era of rule. Inside the castle, visitors can explore its courtyards, galleries, and halls, many of which have been carefully restored. One of the most notable interiors is the Hall of the Barons, where many historic events took place, including the infamous Baronial Conspiracy.

Castel Nuovo houses the Museum of Medieval Art, which features a variety of paintings, sculptures, and historical artifacts, shedding light on the castle's past and its role in the region's political and cultural life. The castle also offers access to several terraces, where visitors can enjoy magnificent views of the city, the harbor, and Mount Vesuvius.

Both Castel dell'Ovo and Castel Nuovo offer an in-depth look at the history and cultural evolution of Naples. Castel dell'Ovo, with its ancient roots and scenic coastal location, provides a quieter experience focused on its role as a military fortress and its legends. Castel Nuovo, with its grand architectural scale and historical significance as a royal residence, is a more expansive exploration of Naples' royal past. Together, these two castles provide visitors with a multifaceted view of Naples' evolution, from ancient times to the Renaissance, and offer unique opportunities to appreciate the city's fascinating history, art, and stunning views of its landscape.

PIAZZA DEL PLEBISCITO AND ROYAL PALACE

Piazza del Plebiscito and the Royal Palace of Naples are two of the city's most important and grandiose landmarks, embodying the historical, political, and architectural significance of Naples. Located in the heart of the city, they are central to understanding the evolution of Naples as a major European city, and they offer visitors a glimpse into the regal past and vibrant present of the city.

- Piazza del Plebiscito

Piazza del Plebiscito is one of Naples' largest and most famous public squares, known for its monumental architecture and significance in the city's history. It is situated at the foot of the

Royal Palace of Naples, framed by two of the city's iconic buildings: the Church of San Francesco di Paola and the Royal Palace. The square is a symbol of Naples' grandeur and its role in Italian unification, as it was the site of key political events, celebrations, and public gatherings.

History and Significance

Piazza del Plebiscito was designed in the late 18th century under the reign of King Ferdinand I of Bourbon. The square's construction began in 1816 and was completed during the Napoleonic era, although it was named after the plebiscite of 1860, when Naples voted to join the Kingdom of Italy. This event marked a significant moment in the city's history, as it became part of a unified Italy, and the square reflects the political and cultural shifts that took place during this time.

Architecture and Design

The square is famous for its spacious layout and neoclassical architecture. The most striking feature of Piazza del Plebiscito is the Church of San Francesco di Paola, which stands at the southern end of the square. The church is a grand example of neoclassical architecture, with a large dome and 34 columns forming a colonnade around the building. The church was inspired by the Pantheon in Rome, and its imposing structure makes it one of Naples' most recognizable landmarks.

On the northern side of the square, the Royal Palace of Naples provides a majestic backdrop, with its historic façade and elegant design. The square itself is often used for public events, concerts, and celebrations, and it serves as a gathering place for locals and tourists alike. The wide-open space allows visitors to take in the impressive views of the palace and the church while enjoying the vibrant atmosphere of one of Naples' most central locations.

Piazza del Plebiscito Today

Today, the square remains a central point for public life in Naples, hosting concerts, political events, and festivals. It is also a popular spot for tourists to gather and explore the surrounding areas, including the Galleria Umberto I, Teatro di San Carlo, and Via Toledo, which leads to the historic center of the city. The square is especially beautiful at night when the buildings are illuminated, creating a magical atmosphere.

- Royal Palace of Naples (Palazzo Reale)

The Royal Palace of Naples is one of the most important and grand palaces in Italy, serving as a symbol of the city's long history as a seat of power and monarchy. Located at the end of Piazza del Plebiscito, the palace has been the residence of many important monarchs, including the Spanish, French, and Bourbon rulers.

History and Significance

The Royal Palace was originally built in the 16th century during the reign of the Spanish Viceroy Pedro Álvarez de Toledo, who commissioned the palace as part of an effort to enhance the city's prestige. Over the years, it was expanded and renovated under different rulers, particularly the Bourbon kings in the 18th century, who transformed it into one of the most lavish royal residences in Europe.

The palace played a central role in the history of Naples, serving as the official residence of the

Spanish and later Bourbon monarchs until the Italian unification in the 19th century. It witnessed numerous political and royal events, including the transition of power and the struggles for control between different European dynasties. Today, the palace is a museum and an important cultural institution in Naples, offering visitors the chance to explore the opulence of royal life in the city.

Architecture and Design

The Royal Palace is a stunning example of Baroque and Neoclassical architecture. Its grand façade, with rustic stonework and elegant detailing, overlooks Piazza del Plebiscito, while the expansive courtyard, lined with statues and fountains, adds to its regal grandeur. The interior of the palace is equally impressive, with rooms designed in lavish styles that reflect the tastes and wealth of the monarchs who once lived there.

One of the most remarkable parts of the palace is the Palazzo Reale's royal apartments, which have been restored to showcase their former splendor. The Throne Room, Hall of Mirrors, and Royal Gardens offer an insight into the life of Naples' royal court, with ornate furnishings, gilded ceilings, and luxurious tapestries. The Palace Chapel, dedicated to St. Januarius, is another stunning space inside the palace, reflecting the strong religious tradition of Naples' ruling families.

Museum and Exhibitions

Today, the Royal Palace is open to the public as part of the National Museum of Naples. Visitors can explore the royal apartments, court rooms, and historical collections, which include period furniture, artwork, and royal memorabilia. The Royal Gardens behind the palace are also open to the public, offering a peaceful retreat with views of the surrounding city.\

- Piazza del Plebiscito and the Royal Palace Today

Together, Piazza del Plebiscito and the Royal Palace form the heart of Naples, attracting both locals and tourists with their beauty and historical importance. The square remains an iconic space for public events, while the Royal Palace continues to be a vital part of Naples' cultural heritage. Whether visiting the palace's museum, strolling through the square, or enjoying a concert in the open-air space, these two landmarks offer visitors a chance to immerse themselves in the city's rich history and vibrant present.

CHAPTER FIVE

CULTURAL AND HISTORICAL HIGHLIGHTS

ARCHAEOLOGICAL MUSEUM OF NAPLES

The Archaeological Museum of Naples (Museo Archeologico Nazionale di Napoli) is one of the world's most renowned museums, particularly for its exceptional collection of ancient Roman, Greek, and Egyptian antiquities. Situated in the heart of Naples, it is an essential stop for those looking to understand the rich history of the region, with a special emphasis on the ancient civilizations that once thrived in the Mediterranean, particularly the cities destroyed by the eruption of Mount Vesuvius in 79 AD.

- History and Significance

The museum was founded in 1816 by the Bourbon monarchy of Naples, following the extensive excavations at Pompeii, Herculaneum, and other ancient sites around the Bay of Naples. Under the direction of the Bourbon kings, who oversaw the excavations, the museum was established to house the immense collection of artifacts discovered during these excavations. Over time, the museum's scope expanded to include important collections from ancient Egypt, Greece, and Etruria, making it one of the most comprehensive archaeological museums in Europe. The museum's holdings span from prehistoric times through to the Renaissance, with an especially impressive array of Roman artifacts.

- Collections and Exhibits

The museum's vast collection is divided into several key areas, each offering a unique insight into the ancient world. Among its most famous collections are:

➢ Pompeii and Herculaneum Collections

The most celebrated feature of the museum is its extensive collection of Pompeian and Herculanean artifacts, drawn from the ruins of the cities that were buried by the eruption of Mount Vesuvius. The museum contains thousands of objects from these sites, offering a rare and remarkably detailed look at Roman life. Highlights include:

1. Frescoes and Mosaics: The museum boasts many stunning examples of Roman wall paintings and intricate floor mosaics that once adorned the homes of Pompeii's citizens. These pieces depict everything from daily life to mythological scenes and are considered masterpieces of Roman art.
2. Household Artifacts: Everyday objects like pottery, glassware, furniture, and personal items give a fascinating glimpse into the domestic lives of ancient Romans.

3. Sculptures: The museum is home to a number of important Roman statues, including portraits of emperors and citizens, as well as representations of Roman gods and heroes. The Hercules of Pompeii is one such notable piece.
4. The Villa of the Mysteries: One of the most celebrated works is a series of frescoes from the Villa of the Mysteries, believed to depict initiation rites for a mysterious cult, perhaps related to the god Dionysus.
5. The Herculaneum Collection is also important, with many objects being more intact due to the different way the town was buried. The preservation of wooden objects, frescoes, and statues offers a vivid and intimate portrait of Roman society.

➢ Egyptian Collection

The museum also holds one of the largest collections of Egyptian artifacts in Italy. Acquired during the 19th century, the Egyptian collection includes a wealth of objects, such as mummies, sarcophagi, funerary masks, statues, and vases, all shedding light on Egypt's ancient religious practices, funerary customs, and daily life. Notable items include mummy portraits and a number of hieroglyphic inscriptions that provide insights into Egyptian writing and culture.

➢ The Farnese Collection

Perhaps the most famous of all the museum's collections is the Farnese Collection, a group of classical sculptures assembled by the Farnese family during the Renaissance. The collection includes iconic works such as the Farnese Hercules, one of the largest and most famous Greek sculptures, and the Farnese Bull, which is an extraordinary marble carving depicting the myth of Dirce. The collection also includes important busts and statues of gods, emperors, and mythological figures.

➢ Greek and Etruscan Collections

The museum's Greek and Etruscan collections provide an in-depth look at the cultures that shaped the Mediterranean before and during the rise of Rome. The Etruscan artifacts include bronze sculptures, urns, and pottery, reflecting the culture of the Etruscans, an ancient civilization in Italy that preceded Rome. The Greek collection features pottery, sculpture, and votive offerings that illustrate the enduring influence of Greek art and mythology on Roman culture.

➤ Mosaic Room

One of the standout features of the museum is its impressive mosaic room, which showcases some of the finest examples of Roman floor mosaics. These mosaics were often found in the homes of wealthy Romans, depicting scenes of mythology, daily life, and nature. The Alexander Mosaic, which depicts the battle between Alexander the Great and Darius III of Persia, is one of the museum's highlights.

- Architecture and Layout

The museum itself is housed in the magnificent Palazzo degli Studi, a Baroque building designed by the architect Giuseppe Cavallini. The palazzo's grand courtyards, frescoed ceilings, and soaring staircases set the stage for an immersive experience in antiquity. The museum's galleries are spacious and well-organized, allowing visitors to journey through the history of the Mediterranean, from Ancient Greece to Roman Egypt, with sections dedicated to specific time periods and geographical regions.

The entrance courtyard of the museum is home to large classical statues, including the famous Farnese Bull, while the museum's mosaic galleries display exquisite examples of Roman craftsmanship. Throughout the museum, visitors are also treated to beautiful frescoed ceilings, marble floors, and grand staircases, which add to the overall experience.

- Visiting the Archaeological Museum of Naples

Located in Piazza Museo Nazionale, the museum is easily accessible and a must-see for anyone visiting Naples. The museum offers a range of guided tours and educational programs, making it a great destination for history buffs, families, and students. Visitors can expect to spend several hours exploring the extensive collections, with plenty of opportunities for learning and reflection.

The museum is open throughout the year, with temporary exhibitions often showcasing additional artifacts and offering a fresh perspective on its collections. The Royal Palace of Naples and Piazza del Plebiscito are nearby, making the museum an integral part of any tour of the historic heart of Naples.

The Archaeological Museum of Naples is one of Italy's premier cultural institutions, offering an unmatched opportunity to explore the ancient world. With its incredible collections from Pompeii, Herculaneum, Egypt, and beyond, the museum provides visitors with a comprehensive understanding of ancient civilizations and their enduring legacy. Whether you are captivated by the preserved ruins of Pompeii, fascinated by Egyptian mummies, or awed by Greek and Roman sculptures, the museum is a treasure trove of history and art. Its impressive architecture and expansive collections make it a highlight of any visit to Naples.

SAN GREGORIO ARMENO

San Gregorio Armeno is one of the most charming and historically significant streets in the historic center of Naples, Italy. Located near the famous Spaccanapoli street, this narrow, picturesque road is renowned for its vibrant atmosphere, rich history, and connection to the traditional Neapolitan Nativity scene (presepe) culture.

- Historical Significance

San Gregorio Armeno takes its name from the Church of San Gregorio Armeno, a stunning baroque church founded in the 8th century and dedicated to Saint Gregory the Great. The church, which is an important religious site in Naples, is noted for its ornate architecture and beautiful interior. However, it is the surrounding street and its cultural heritage that has made this area famous worldwide.

Historically, San Gregorio Armeno has been a center for artisan craftsmanship, particularly in the creation of Nativity scenes. The tradition of building and displaying Nativity scenes is deeply embedded in Neapolitan culture, and the artisans of San Gregorio Armeno have been producing intricate figures and scenes for centuries. The street is lined with numerous small shops and workshops where you can find handcrafted figurines, including representations of the Holy Family, angels, shepherds, and various Neapolitan characters, all painted and sculpted with incredible attention to detail.

- The Art of the Presepe (Nativity Scene)

San Gregorio Armeno is especially famous for its presepe tradition, which dates back to the 17th century. Neapolitan Nativity scenes are renowned for their realism, often incorporating not only biblical figures but also scenes of everyday life in Naples, with figures such as bakers, street vendors, musicians, and even politicians. The street is home to the artisan workshops that continue to produce these highly detailed and often personalized figures.

During the Christmas season, San Gregorio Armeno becomes even more lively and magical, as the shops display their Nativity scenes in full grandeur, attracting tourists and locals alike. The street is crowded with people browsing the intricate figurines and enjoying the festive atmosphere, making it a must-visit during the holiday season. Visitors can purchase a variety of figures to complete their own Nativity scenes, from small, traditional pieces to larger, more elaborate displays.

- The Church of San Gregorio Armeno

The Church of San Gregorio Armeno itself is a masterpiece of Baroque architecture, with an impressive façade and a richly decorated interior. The church was originally founded in the 9th century by St. Gregory of Nazianzus, but it was rebuilt in its current Baroque style in the 17th century. Inside, visitors can admire frescoes, marble altars, and a beautiful ceiling painted by the renowned artist Giovanni Lanfranco. The church's significance goes beyond its architectural beauty; it also plays an important role in the religious life of the city and is home to the Monastic Order of Benedictine Nuns.

- Visiting San Gregorio Armeno

San Gregorio Armeno is located in the heart of Naples' historic center, easily accessible from Spaccanapoli and other popular attractions such as the Naples Cathedral and the Museum of San Martino. Visitors can wander the cobblestone streets, browse the artisan shops, and enjoy the rich cultural and artistic atmosphere that permeates this area.

While San Gregorio Armeno is a must-visit during the Christmas season, the street also offers a glimpse into the traditional craftsmanship and daily life of Naples year-round. Even outside of the holiday period, the shops remain open, allowing visitors to purchase unique souvenirs and appreciate the fine artistry of the presepe makers.

San Gregorio Armeno is a beautiful and historically rich street that encapsulates the spirit of Naples, blending art, religion, and tradition. Whether you're interested in the centuries-old art of the Nativity scene, the architectural splendor of the Church of San Gregorio Armeno, or simply soaking in the vibrant atmosphere of one of Naples' most iconic streets, San Gregorio Armeno offers an unforgettable experience. It is a perfect place to witness the artistic and cultural heritage of Naples, especially for those who want to take home a piece of the city's festive spirit.

TEATRO DI SAN CARLO

The Teatro di San Carlo is one of the most prestigious and historic opera houses in the world, located in the heart of Naples, Italy. Known for its rich history, architectural beauty, and exceptional acoustics, it is a must-visit cultural landmark for anyone interested in classical music, opera, and the arts. As one of the oldest opera houses still in operation, Teatro di San Carlo has played a significant role in the development of opera and remains a central venue for musical performances in Naples today.

- History and Significance

The Teatro di San Carlo was inaugurated in 1737 by the Bourbon king Charles of Bourbon, who commissioned the theater as part of his efforts to elevate Naples as a cultural hub in Europe. Designed by the architect Giovanni Antonio Medrano and built by the Neapolitan engineer Francesco Collecini, the theater was originally constructed to rival the grand opera houses of Europe, such as the Vienna State Opera and the Paris Opera. Its creation was also part of a broader cultural revival during the reign of the Bourbon dynasty in Naples.

At the time of its opening, the Teatro di San Carlo was one of the largest and most advanced opera houses in Europe. It quickly became an important center for opera, attracting world-class composers, musicians, and opera singers. Over the centuries, the theater has hosted numerous iconic performances and world premieres, becoming a symbol of Neapolitan cultural heritage.

- Architecture and Interior

The architecture of Teatro di San Carlo reflects the grandeur and elegance of the 18th century. Built in the Baroque style, the theater features a stunning façade adorned with columns and statues, giving it an imposing presence on the Piazza del Plebiscito. The theater's interior is equally magnificent, with an auditorium that can accommodate around 1,300 spectators.

The theater's most striking feature is its horseshoe-shaped auditorium, a design that was revolutionary at the time and became a model for other European opera houses. The interior is decorated with gold leaf, frescoes, and intricate carvings, creating an opulent atmosphere. The grand chandeliers and the royal box, where the king and high-ranking officials would sit, add to the splendor of the space. The ceiling fresco, painted by Giuseppe Cammarano, depicts a scene from Greek mythology, further enhancing the theater's artistic appeal.

The acoustics of Teatro di San Carlo are renowned worldwide. The theater was designed with sound quality in mind, and even today, it is considered one of the best venues for opera and classical music performances due to its exceptional acoustics, which allow the smallest nuances of the music to be heard clearly from any seat in the house.

- Performances and Cultural Impact

Teatro di San Carlo has been the site of many historic performances and premieres, cementing its reputation as a leading opera house. In the 18th and 19th centuries, the theater hosted world premieres of works by some of Italy's greatest composers, including Giuseppe Verdi, Giacomo Puccini, and Vincenzo Bellini. Many famous opera singers and musicians, including Luciano

Pavarotti, Maria Callas, and Placido Domingo, have graced the stage of San Carlo.

Today, the theater continues to offer a rich program of opera, ballet, and classical music performances. It is the home of the Teatro di San Carlo Opera Company and serves as an important cultural institution in Naples. Visitors to the theater can enjoy a variety of productions, from classic operas to contemporary works, as well as ballet performances and concerts.

- Visiting Teatro di San Carlo

Visitors to Teatro di San Carlo can experience its beauty and history in several ways. The theater offers guided tours that take guests through its rich history, showcasing its stunning architecture, lavish interiors, and important cultural legacy. These tours are an excellent way to learn about the theater's significance and discover the stories behind some of its most memorable performances.

In addition to attending performances, visitors can also explore the theater's museum, which houses historical artifacts related to the theater's past, including costumes, set designs, and memorabilia from past performances.

For those who are fortunate enough to be in Naples during one of its performances, attending a concert, opera, or ballet at Teatro di San Carlo is an unforgettable experience. The grand atmosphere, exceptional acoustics, and world-class productions make it a highlight of any visit to Naples.

The Teatro di San Carlo is a true gem of Naples, rich in history, culture, and artistic achievement. As one of the oldest and most important opera houses in Europe, it remains a vibrant center for the performing arts, offering an exceptional experience for music lovers and history enthusiasts alike. Whether you are attending a performance, taking a guided tour, or simply admiring its architectural beauty, Teatro di San Carlo is an essential part of any visit to Naples, representing the city's enduring contribution to the world of music and culture.

LOCAL ART AND CONTEMPORARY GALLERIES

Naples is a city that beautifully blends its rich cultural history with a vibrant and ever-evolving contemporary art scene. Known for its centuries-old traditions in craftsmanship, Naples is also home to a dynamic community of artists who are reshaping the city's artistic landscape. Whether you're drawn to traditional local art or cutting-edge contemporary works, Naples offers a wide variety of galleries and art spaces where visitors can explore a diverse range of artistic expressions.

- Local Art and Traditional Crafts

Neapolitan art is deeply rooted in the city's heritage, which has been influenced by a blend of Greek, Roman, and Renaissance traditions. The city's artisan workshops continue to produce works that reflect this rich history, with presepe (Nativity scene) figures being a particularly significant craft. These intricately sculpted figurines, often portraying both biblical scenes and aspects of daily life in Naples, are a unique aspect of the local art culture. The San Gregorio Armeno street, for example, is famous for its numerous shops where visitors can see these figures being hand-carved and painted, offering a tangible connection to the city's artistic past.

Additionally, ceramics and woodwork are prominent traditional crafts in Naples. The craftsmanship in hand-painted tiles and ornate wood sculptures speaks to the enduring influence of Naples' artistic heritage, making these works highly sought after by collectors and visitors alike.

- Contemporary Art Galleries

While Naples holds strong to its traditional roots, the city has also become a key player in the contemporary art world, with a number of galleries and institutions promoting modern art. The vibrant art scene in Naples is marked by a fusion of international artistic movements with local themes, often addressing issues of identity, culture, and social change.

> Museo Madre (Museum of Contemporary Art in Naples): The Museo Madre stands as Naples' premier contemporary art museum, housed in a beautifully restored historic

palace. It showcases a wide range of contemporary works from both international artists and Italian talents, covering everything from painting and sculpture to digital art and video installations. The museum hosts numerous rotating exhibitions, making it a central institution for those interested in exploring the most innovative and thought-provoking contemporary art.

- Galleria d'Arte Contemporanea (GAC): Located in the historic center of Naples, GAC is another key venue that promotes experimental works by local and international artists. The gallery is known for its diverse exhibitions that include photography, video art, and mixed-media installations, often engaging with urban culture and social issues.

- PAN | Palazzo delle Arti Napoli: Another important venue is PAN, the Palazzo delle Arti Napoli, which hosts a wide variety of contemporary exhibitions. With its focus on both traditional and innovative forms of artistic expression, PAN is an excellent place to discover cutting-edge works that engage with the cultural pulse of Naples.

- Studio Trisorio: A renowned contemporary art gallery, Studio Trisorio has played a vital role in Naples' modern art scene by exhibiting a wide range of contemporary works, from installation art to photography. The gallery's focus on avant-garde and conceptual works makes it a must-visit for those interested in pushing the boundaries of art.

- La Galleria Alberto Peola: Known for its high-quality exhibitions of contemporary art, La Galleria Alberto Peola focuses on conceptual and experimental works that encourage new forms of artistic expression. The gallery's exhibitions often delve into themes that provoke dialogue and thought, offering visitors a deeper understanding of modern art.

- Street Art and Public Installations

Naples also boasts a thriving street art scene, where the city's walls and public spaces have become canvases for both local and international artists. In neighborhoods like Vico Ferrovia, Quartieri Spagnoli, and Sanità, murals and graffiti art transform the urban landscape, adding layers of color, culture, and social commentary to the streets.

One of the most exciting aspects of Naples' street art scene is its community-driven approach, with local initiatives commissioning murals that reflect the identity of the neighborhood. These artworks often depict elements of daily life in Naples, historical references, or political statements, making them a reflection of the city's diverse and evolving identity.

In addition to street art, Naples is home to numerous public art installations that further enhance the city's artistic appeal. Sculptures, projections, and immersive art experiences are placed in various public squares, streets, and parks, inviting interaction and engagement from the public. Events like "Street Art Naples" festivals have made these public spaces dynamic showcases for both established and emerging street artists.

- Art Festivals and Events

Naples is a city that celebrates art in all its forms, and several annual events highlight its thriving contemporary scene.

> Naples Contemporary Art Week: This event is an essential part of Naples' art calendar, bringing together numerous galleries, museums, and independent spaces to showcase contemporary art. Visitors can attend exhibitions, openings, and

performances throughout the city, gaining a broad view of the local and international contemporary art scene.

- ➤ Artissima Napoli: Another key event is Artissima, an international art fair that takes place annually, attracting galleries and artists from across the globe. The fair features contemporary works in a variety of mediums and is a highlight for collectors, curators, and art enthusiasts.

- ➤ Teatro San Carlo's Contemporary Art Exhibitions: Although renowned for its opera and classical performances, Teatro San Carlo also hosts contemporary art exhibitions in its lobby and other areas. These events bring together the worlds of performing arts and visual arts, creating a unique cultural experience.

Naples offers a fascinating and multifaceted art scene, blending traditional craftsmanship with the bold innovations of contemporary art. From the intricate presepe figures to the dynamic exhibitions at institutions like Museo Madre and PAN, Naples is a city where art continues to evolve and thrive. Its street art culture and public installations add to the city's charm, while the annual art events bring the community together to celebrate the power of creative expression. Whether you are a seasoned art lover or simply curious about exploring Naples' artistic legacy, the city offers an unforgettable journey through its rich and diverse art world.

CHAPTER SIX

FOOD AND CULINARY EXPERIENCES

THE BIRTHPLACE OF PIZZA

Naples is widely regarded as the birthplace of pizza, a dish that has become beloved worldwide. The origins of pizza in Naples can be traced back to the 18th century, when the city, already a vibrant hub of culture and commerce, began to shape this iconic food into the dish we recognize today.

- Early Beginnings

The origins of pizza in Naples are linked to the peasant food culture of southern Italy. The region's fertile land, combined with its access to fresh, local ingredients such as tomatoes, mozzarella, olive oil, and herbs, made it an ideal setting for the creation of a simple, yet flavorful dish. Early versions of pizza were more akin to flatbreads topped with various local ingredients, but it was in Naples that pizza began to take its recognizable form.

The modern pizza as we know it, with a round dough base topped with tomatoes, mozzarella, and basil, was born out of this combination of local ingredients and culinary tradition. Tomatoes, which arrived from the Americas in the 16th century, were initially thought to be poisonous but became a popular ingredient in the 17th century, especially in Naples. This addition to flatbreads eventually evolved into the familiar pizza.

- The Iconic Margherita Pizza

The most famous pizza to emerge from Naples is the Margherita, which is said to have been created in 1889. According to legend, the pizza was invented by a Neapolitan pizzaiolo (pizza maker) named Raffaele Esposito, who was asked to create a special dish for Queen Margherita of Savoy during her visit to Naples. Esposito prepared a pizza with toppings that represented the colors of the Italian flag: red tomatoes, white mozzarella, and green basil. The queen was so impressed by the dish that it was named in her honor, becoming Pizza Margherita.

While the story of Queen Margherita's visit is widely celebrated, it's important to note that the pizza was already a popular food in Naples long before this event. Nevertheless, the Margherita pizza's association with royalty helped cement its place as the quintessential Neapolitan pizza.

- Traditional Neapolitan Pizza

Today, Neapolitan pizza is a symbol of Naples and is protected by tradition. In 1984, the Associazione Verace Pizza Napoletana (True Neapolitan Pizza Association) was established to preserve the authenticity of Neapolitan pizza. According to the association's standards, a true pizza napoletana must be made with specific ingredients: the dough must be hand-kneaded, the crust should be thin and slightly raised around the edges, and the pizza should be cooked in a wood-fired oven at a high temperature for about 90 seconds. The ingredients must include San Marzano tomatoes (grown in the volcanic soil of Mount Vesuvius), Mozzarella di Bufala (buffalo mozzarella), and fresh basil.

The traditional pizzas in Naples include not only the famous Margherita but also Pizza Marinara (a simple pizza with tomato, garlic, oregano, and olive oil) and other variations that highlight the rich flavors of the region. Neapolitan pizzerias have earned a reputation for their commitment to tradition, with some even being awarded UNESCO Intangible Cultural Heritage status for their role in preserving the art of pizza-making.

- Pizza and the Neapolitan Culture

Pizza has become an integral part of Neapolitan identity. It's more than just a meal; it's a part of daily life. In Naples, pizza is often enjoyed with friends or family, typically eaten at a local pizzeria, and often paired with a refreshing drink. The pizzerias of Naples are famous for their traditional ovens and the way pizza is prepared in a fast, skilled manner by expert pizzaiolos. Eating pizza in Naples is an experience that goes beyond just the flavors—it's about the ambiance, the skill, and the pride that comes with making and eating this iconic dish.

- Global Influence

As Naples is the birthplace of pizza, the city's influence on the dish extends far beyond its borders. Italian immigrants brought their love for pizza to countries like the United States, where it became an enormous hit in cities like New York and Chicago. Over time, different regional variations of pizza emerged, such as New York-style pizza, deep-dish pizza, and many others.

However, no matter how far pizza has spread or how many variations exist, the Neapolitan pizza remains the gold standard, with its combination of fresh ingredients, simple flavors, and dedication to tradition.

Naples is undeniably the birthplace of pizza, and the city's long-standing tradition of pizza-making has shaped the dish into the global phenomenon it is today. The Margherita pizza, created in honor of Queen Margherita, continues to stand as the symbol of Neapolitan pizza, while the city's pizzerias remain the best places to experience the art of pizza-making in its purest form. Whether you are enjoying a classic pizza at one of the many historic pizzerias in Naples or savoring a slice in a distant corner of the world, the essence of Naples' culinary legacy lives on through pizza.

TRADITIONAL NEAPOLITAN CUISINE

Traditional Neapolitan cuisine is a vibrant and flavorful reflection of Naples' rich history, geographic location, and cultural influences. Situated between the mountains and the sea, Naples has access to an abundance of fresh, local ingredients that have shaped its culinary traditions. The cuisine is characterized by its simplicity, bold flavors, and an emphasis on quality ingredients. From the iconic pizza to pasta dishes, seafood, and desserts, Neapolitan food offers an unforgettable culinary experience.

- Pizza Napoletana

Arguably the most famous culinary creation to emerge from Naples is pizza. Pizza Napoletana is a cherished part of the city's identity. The most iconic variety is Pizza Margherita, created with a simple base of San Marzano tomatoes, Mozzarella di Bufala (buffalo mozzarella), extra virgin olive oil, and fresh basil, all atop a thin, charred dough. This combination of fresh, high-quality ingredients reflects the agricultural wealth of the region and is central to Neapolitan pizza tradition. Another beloved classic is Pizza Marinara, a simpler version topped with tomato sauce, garlic, oregano, and olive oil. Both versions exemplify the commitment to fresh, simple ingredients and the artistry of pizza-making in Naples.

- Pasta Dishes

Neapolitan cuisine features an array of delicious pasta dishes, many of which highlight the region's abundance of fresh ingredients, including tomatoes, seafood, and local herbs. Some of the standout pasta dishes include:

> Spaghetti alle Vongole: A classic Neapolitan dish consisting of spaghetti served with clams, garlic, olive oil, and white wine. The

dish captures the fresh flavors of the sea and is a beloved staple in Naples.

- Linguine alle Cozze: Linguine pasta served with mussels, garlic, tomato sauce, and a splash of white wine. It's another great example of the city's love for seafood, with simple yet bold flavors.

- Gnocchi alla Sorrentina: A comforting dish of potato gnocchi baked in a rich sauce of tomatoes, Mozzarella di Bufala, and basil. This dish represents the rustic, hearty side of Neapolitan cooking, often served in family-style portions.

- Pasta e Fagioli: A filling and flavorful dish of pasta and beans, typically served with a light tomato sauce and olive oil. It's a perfect example of the humble, peasant roots of Neapolitan cuisine, where simple ingredients are transformed into a hearty, satisfying meal.

- Seafood

Given Naples' coastal location, seafood plays a central role in its culinary tradition. The city's seafood dishes often emphasize fresh, seasonal ingredients and are prepared in simple ways to highlight the natural flavors. Some of the most popular seafood dishes include:

- Frittura di Paranza: A plate of fried small fish, often including anchovies, sardines, and squid. The fish are lightly battered and fried, creating a crispy, flavorful treat that's often served with a squeeze of lemon.

- Baccalà alla Napoletana: Salted codfish prepared with tomatoes, garlic, olives, and capers. This dish is a traditional way of preserving cod and offers a rich, savory taste that's typical of Neapolitan cooking.

- Insalata di Mare: A refreshing seafood salad made with a mix of shrimp, octopus, squid, and other shellfish, dressed with lemon, olive oil, and a sprinkling of parsley. It's a light and bright dish that captures the flavors of the Mediterranean Sea.

- Meat Dishes

While seafood dominates much of Neapolitan cuisine, there are several classic meat dishes that are also integral to the culinary tradition. These dishes showcase the region's emphasis on simple yet flavorful cooking techniques. Some examples include:

> Polpette (Neapolitan Meatballs): Meatballs made from a combination of beef and pork, seasoned with garlic, parsley, parmesan, and bread crumbs, often served in a rich tomato sauce. This dish is a comforting and popular choice, often enjoyed with pasta or as a main course.

- Agnello al Forno: Roast lamb prepared with garlic, rosemary, and olive oil, and usually served with roasted potatoes. It's a dish typically served during holidays or special occasions, showcasing the region's ability to create flavorful and tender meat dishes.

- Braciola di Maiale: A classic Neapolitan dish made with pork chops, which are braised with tomatoes, onions, and garlic until tender. This savory dish is full of rich flavors and is often served with side dishes such as potatoes or vegetables.

- Desserts

Neapolitan desserts are just as rich and flavorful as the savory dishes. The city is famous for its sweet treats, many of which incorporate local ingredients like ricotta, chocolate, and citrus. Some must-try desserts include:

- Sfogliatella: A traditional Neapolitan pastry, sfogliatella comes in two forms: riccia (flaky) and frolla (soft). The pastry is filled with a sweet ricotta filling and often flavored with citrus or vanilla. It's a perfect example of the city's pastry craftsmanship.

- Pastiera Napoletana: A traditional Easter dessert, pastiera is a rich ricotta and wheat pie flavored with orange blossom water and cinnamon. It's often served during the Easter holiday but is enjoyed year-round.

- Delizia al Limone: A light and refreshing dessert made with lemon, often prepared as a soft cake soaked in lemon syrup and topped with a lemon cream. The lemon, a staple ingredient in the Amalfi Coast region, is a central feature of this delightful treat.

Traditional Neapolitan cuisine is a celebration of fresh, high-quality ingredients, time-honored cooking techniques, and a deep connection to the region's history. The iconic Pizza Napoletana, with its simple yet delicious toppings, is a cornerstone of the city's food culture, while pasta dishes, seafood, and meat dishes showcase the diversity and depth of flavors that define Neapolitan cooking. Add to that the delicious array of desserts, and it's clear that Naples is a food lover's paradise, offering a true taste of Italy's culinary heritage.

STREET FOOD AND LOCAL MARKETS

Street food and local markets are an essential part of the cultural fabric of Naples. The city's vibrant street food scene reflects its rich culinary traditions, offering visitors the chance to sample delicious, authentic dishes that are prepared fresh and often enjoyed on the go. Neapolitan street food is all about simplicity, flavor, and using locally sourced ingredients. From savory treats to sweet indulgences, Naples offers an array of mouth-watering options that reflect the essence of its cuisine.

- Street Food in Naples
- Pizza Margherita by the Slice

While Naples is the birthplace of pizza, it's also home to a more casual way of enjoying it: pizza by the slice. Known as "pizza a portafoglio", which translates to "pizza to fold," this street food is served in large slices, folded in half like a wallet. It's a quick and satisfying meal for anyone on the go. Many pizzerias and street vendors sell pizza in this way, making it a popular snack among locals and tourists alike.

- Pizza Fritta (Fried Pizza)

Another beloved street food in Naples is pizza fritta, a deep-fried version of pizza dough stuffed with a variety of fillings. The dough is folded over and then fried until golden and crispy. Common fillings include ricotta cheese, mozzarella, tomato, and salami, though there are many variations. It's a deliciously indulgent snack, perfect for satisfying a craving for something crispy, cheesy, and savory.

➤ Cuoppo

Cuoppo is a traditional paper cone filled with a mix of fried seafood or fried vegetables. This street food is especially popular in the coastal areas of Naples. A typical cuoppo might include fried shrimp, anchovies, squid, zucchini, and eggplant. The crunchy, golden pieces are served with a wedge of lemon and sometimes a dash of salt or pepper. It's a perfect snack for those looking to enjoy fresh, crispy seafood while exploring the city.

➤ Frittatina di Pasta

Frittatina di pasta is a beloved Neapolitan street food made from leftover pasta that is breaded, deep-fried, and shaped into a patty. The pasta is usually cooked with a rich ragù or bolognese sauce, then mixed with cheese and peas before being coated in breadcrumbs and fried. It's a savory snack that combines the flavors of pasta with the satisfying crunch of the fried exterior.

➤ Panino Napoletano (Neapolitan Sandwich)

Neapolitan street food also includes delicious sandwiches made with local bread, such as cacciatorino (a type of sausage) and mozzarella di bufala. Panino Napoletano might also feature salami, prosciutto, or other cured meats, along with fresh tomatoes and cheese. These sandwiches are perfect for a quick and satisfying bite.

- Local Markets in Naples

Neapolitan markets are not only a place to shop for fresh ingredients, but also offer an immersive experience into the city's vibrant food culture. The local markets are bustling with activity, filled with colorful stalls offering everything from fresh produce to cheese, meat, seafood, and sweets. These markets are where locals shop for their daily meals, and visitors can get a true taste of the region's flavors and ingredients.

➢ Mercato di Porta Nolana

One of the most famous markets in Naples is Mercato di Porta Nolana, located near the Porta Nolana area. This lively market is known for its fresh seafood, which comes straight from the nearby Bay of Naples. You'll find stalls selling everything from fresh fish and squid to clams and lobsters. In addition to seafood, the market also offers a wide variety of fruits, vegetables, and local products like cured meats, cheeses, and spices. It's an excellent spot to explore and sample some of the freshest ingredients Naples has to offer.

➢ Mercato di Pignasecca

Another iconic market is Mercato di Pignasecca, one of the oldest and most famous food markets in Naples. Located in the heart of the historic center, this bustling market is known for its vibrant atmosphere and wide variety of products. You can find fresh fruits and vegetables, traditional Neapolitan cheeses like Caciocavallo and Mozzarella di Bufala, meats, cured sausages, and even freshly made pasta. It's also a great place to buy local street food, such as sfogliatella (a sweet pastry), fried pizza, or arancini (stuffed rice balls).

➢ Mercato di Sant'Antonio Abate

The Mercato di Sant'Antonio Abate is a popular market located near the Stazione Centrale. It offers a wide variety of fresh food, including produce, meats, cheeses, and seafood. The market is known for its historical significance, dating back to the 19th century, and it has remained a vital place for locals to gather fresh ingredients. It's also an excellent place to find street food, such as frittatina and pizza a portafoglio.

- Mercato della Vucciria

A short distance from the center, the Mercato della Vucciria is another lively market that's famous for its seafood and fresh local produce. Here, visitors can sample a wide variety of fresh pasta, cheeses, and cured meats, as well as more unusual Neapolitan foods like soppressata (a type of dry salami) and provola cheese.

Street food and local markets are an essential part of the Neapolitan experience, offering visitors the chance to enjoy the freshest, most authentic flavors the city has to offer. Whether it's grabbing a quick bite of pizza fritta from a street vendor or exploring the vibrant markets like Porta Nolana and Pignasecca, Naples is a city where food is always around the corner, ready to be savored. The combination of traditional street foods, fresh local ingredients, and the lively market atmosphere creates an immersive, sensory-rich culinary experience that should not be missed when visiting Naples.

FINE DINING AND WINE EXPERIENCES

Fine dining and wine experiences in Naples offer a sophisticated and memorable way to explore the city's rich culinary heritage. While Naples is often celebrated for its street food and rustic flavors, it also boasts an impressive array of fine dining restaurants and gourmet wine experiences that showcase the region's ability to combine tradition with innovation. Whether it's enjoying a meal at a Michelin-starred restaurant or sipping on some of the finest wines from the region, there's something for every food enthusiast looking to indulge in Naples' elevated culinary scene.

- Fine Dining in Naples

Michelin-Starred Restaurants Naples is home to several Michelin-starred restaurants, where guests can experience the perfect marriage of creativity, quality ingredients, and exceptional service. One of the city's most renowned fine dining establishments is Restaurant Palazzo Petrucci, which holds a Michelin star for its inventive take on classic Neapolitan cuisine. Known for its elegant atmosphere and sophisticated dishes, Palazzo Petrucci offers a seasonal menu that combines traditional flavors with modern techniques, using locally sourced ingredients and fresh seafood.

Another celebrated Michelin-starred spot is Il Comandante, located on the rooftop of the Romeo Hotel. The restaurant is known for its stunning views of the Gulf of Naples and Mount Vesuvius, providing a spectacular setting for enjoying high-end, contemporary Italian cuisine. The innovative dishes, created by Chef Salvatore Bianco, are carefully crafted using the finest local and international ingredients, offering a refined and multi-sensory dining experience.

Contemporary Italian Cuisine For those looking for contemporary Italian fine dining, La Bersagliera is a must-visit. Situated in a historical building in the heart of the city, this restaurant offers an elegant atmosphere and a menu that blends traditional Neapolitan flavors with modern culinary techniques. Expect creative interpretations of classic dishes like risotto, seafood, and meat-based dishes prepared with an innovative twist.

Neapolitan Culinary Tradition Meets Fine Dining For an authentic taste of Naples in a refined setting, Le Figlie di Iorio offers a perfect balance between classic Neapolitan dishes and elegant presentation. Known for its intimate ambiance and attentive service, this restaurant serves high-end versions of traditional meals, such as spaghetti alle vongole and gnocchi alla sorrentina, elevated with fine wines and intricate plating.

- Wine Experiences in Naples

The Campania region, where Naples is located, is home to some of Italy's finest wines, and Naples offers a variety of opportunities to explore and enjoy these exceptional local vintages.

Vino Nobile di Montepulciano, Greco di Tufo, and Lacryma Christi The wines of Campania are rich in history, with centuries-old traditions of winemaking that continue to thrive today. Lacryma Christi, one of the most iconic wines of Naples, is grown on the volcanic slopes of Mount Vesuvius. This wine comes in both red and white varieties, offering complex flavors with a mineral quality due to the volcanic soil. The region is also known for Greco di Tufo, a white wine made from a native grape variety that produces crisp, citrusy wines with a distinct floral note, and Fiano di Avellino, another local white wine with a fuller body and honeyed richness.

Wine Tasting Experiences There are several vineyards and wineries in the surrounding

Campania region that offer wine-tasting experiences. One such place is Cantina del Vesuvio, located on the slopes of Mount Vesuvius. Here, visitors can sample the region's famous Lacryma Christi, while learning about the history of winemaking on the volcano and the unique characteristics of the soil that influence the wine's flavor. The winery offers tours through its vineyards, where guests can enjoy panoramic views of the Bay of Naples and taste wines paired with local cheeses and meats.

Another notable winery in the region is Feudi di San Gregorio, which offers guided tours and tastings of its renowned wines, including the Fiano di Avellino and Aglianico varieties. The estate is known for its modern winemaking techniques that respect the traditions of the region while creating wines that are internationally recognized for their quality.

For a truly unique experience, consider taking a wine and food pairing class. Many restaurants in Naples offer curated tasting menus that pair traditional dishes with wines from the region. This is a fantastic way to discover how the flavors of Naples and Campania are complemented by locally produced wines.

- Wine Bars and Enotecas

For a more casual but equally enjoyable wine experience, Naples has a number of excellent wine bars and enotecas where visitors can taste a wide selection of local wines. Enoteca Belledonne is one of the most popular spots for wine lovers in the city. Located in the historic center, this cozy wine bar features an extensive list of local wines, including rare and vintage bottles. The knowledgeable staff can guide you through the selection, helping you choose the perfect wine to pair with a plate of cheese, charcuterie, or other small plates.

Another great wine bar is Vineria San Sebastiano, which offers a carefully curated list of wines from across the Campania region, as well as light bites such as olives, cheese, and salami. The relaxed atmosphere makes it an ideal spot for unwinding after a day of sightseeing while sipping on a glass of Lacryma Christi.

- Wine and Dine with Views

For those looking to enjoy both fine dining and exceptional views, Terrazza dell'Orologio is a must-visit. Located in the Grand Hotel Vesuvio, this rooftop restaurant and bar offer sweeping views of the Bay of Naples, Mount Vesuvius, and the coastline. The menu features a mix of traditional Neapolitan dishes and Mediterranean-inspired fare, with a selection of local wines to complement each course. Dining here is a truly luxurious experience, combining delicious food, fine wine, and breathtaking views.

Naples offers an array of fine dining experiences and wine tastings that elevate the city's culinary offerings. From Michelin-starred restaurants and contemporary Italian cuisine to wine bars and vineyard tours, the city provides endless opportunities to indulge in world-class food and wine. Whether you're savoring a creative dish at a fine dining establishment or exploring the wines of Campania, a trip to Naples promises a memorable gastronomic journey that showcases the best of local flavors, wines, and traditions.

CHAPTER SEVEN

SHOPPING IN NAPLES

UNIQUE BOUTIQUES AND ARTISAN SHOPS

Naples is a city brimming with unique boutiques and artisan shops, where visitors can find one-of-a-kind treasures that reflect the rich cultural heritage and craftsmanship of the region. The city's historic center is filled with small, family-run shops, artisan workshops, and independent boutiques, offering everything from handmade jewelry and custom leather goods to traditional ceramics and local delicacies. Shopping in Naples is an immersive experience, where you can discover the true essence of Neapolitan craftsmanship and style.

- Handcrafted Ceramics

Naples is renowned for its ceramic art, particularly the vibrant majolica pottery that has been produced in the region for centuries. The city's artisan ceramic shops showcase a stunning array of hand-painted tiles, vases, bowls, and decorative pieces, each reflecting the colorful spirit of Neapolitan culture.

One of the most famous areas for ceramic shopping is Vico dei Maiolicari, a narrow street in the historic center where several artisan shops line the road, offering handmade ceramics. Many of these pieces feature traditional blue and yellow motifs, inspired by the Mediterranean coast, as well as floral patterns and scenes of local life. Ceramiche Lamberti is a well-known ceramic shop that offers high-quality pieces, while Ceramiche de Simone creates hand-painted designs that draw on Neapolitan folklore and history.

For more contemporary designs, Raffaele Ceramics is a boutique that blends traditional techniques with modern aesthetics, offering beautifully crafted pieces with a more artistic edge.

- Custom Leather Goods

Naples is also famous for its tradition of crafting leather goods, and visitors will find an abundance of shops offering handcrafted leather bags, wallets, belts, and shoes. The city's artisan leather shops focus on quality craftsmanship, with leather sourced from the best suppliers and products made by hand using traditional techniques.

Pelletteria Napolitana is a classic example of a high-quality leather goods store in Naples, where you can find everything from luxury handbags to personalized accessories. This boutique is known for its attention to detail and commitment to producing timeless leather products. Another popular option is Chicco Pelle, which offers custom-made leather bags and accessories that are both stylish and durable. Here, you can request bespoke items tailored to your exact specifications, creating a truly personalized shopping experience.

- Jewelry and Traditional Goldsmithing

Naples has a long-standing tradition of goldsmithing and fine jewelry making, dating back to ancient times. The city is known for its intricate gold jewelry, often adorned with cameos, corals, and precious stones, as well as unique design pieces inspired by the region's history and natural beauty.

One of the most famous streets for jewelry shopping in Naples is Via San Gregorio Armeno, a bustling road in the historic center known for its artisan shops that sell Neapolitan nativity scenes and handmade jewelry. Many of the shops here specialize in cameos, a traditional form of jewelry in which delicate portraits or scenes are carved into shells, coral, or stone. Gioielleria Spadafora and Gioielleria Assunta are two examples of high-end jewelers where you can find exquisite gold and silver pieces crafted by skilled artisans.

For a more modern twist on traditional goldsmithing, Francesco Gatti Gioielli offers contemporary designs that incorporate elements of Naples' cultural history while embracing sleek, modern aesthetics.

- Neapolitan Fashion and Boutiques

Naples is home to a growing fashion scene, with boutiques that offer chic and elegant clothing, often with a Mediterranean flair. The city's tailored fashion blends classic Italian craftsmanship with a contemporary edge, offering stylish, high-quality pieces for both men and women.

Antica Sartoria is a well-known boutique that specializes in high-end Italian fashion with a distinctly Neapolitan influence. The boutique is famous for its handmade linen shirts, tailored suits, and colorful accessories that reflect the vibrant spirit of Naples. Another great stop for fashion lovers is Mario d'Antonio, a boutique offering bespoke tailoring and exclusive collections of Italian-made clothing, as well as luxury leather and silk scarves.

For a more relaxed, bohemian style, Ciccio Napoli is a quirky boutique known for its eclectic mix of vintage fashion, handcrafted jewelry, and local artisan products. The store offers a selection of unique pieces that blend old-world charm with modern style, perfect for visitors looking for something off the beaten path.

- Local Delicacies and Specialty Foods

In Naples, local markets and food shops offer the perfect opportunity to take home a taste of the city's rich culinary heritage. The markets are filled with specialty products like local olive oils, cured meats, and fresh cheeses, while the food boutiques offer unique, handmade pasta, chocolates, and sweet treats that are perfect for gifting or enjoying at home.

Antica Tradizione is a charming shop in the historic center where you can find Neapolitan pastries like sfogliatella, pastiera, and delizia al limone. The store also offers a wide selection of local chocolates and confectioneries, perfect for indulging in the city's sweet side. For local cheeses and cured meats, Salumeria Sannino offers an excellent selection of Neapolitan cheeses like Caciocavallo and Mozzarella di Bufala, as well as locally produced salami and prosciutto.

Another must-visit for food lovers is Caffè Gambrinus, an iconic Neapolitan café known for its coffee beans and local pastries, where you can also buy coffee and sweet treats to bring home. Gran Caffè La Caffettiera offers not only delicious coffee but also a selection of artisanal liqueurs, including Limoncello, which is made from the region's famous lemons.

- Art and Craft Galleries

Naples is also home to several art galleries and craft shops where you can find paintings, sculptures, and handcrafted items that reflect the city's artistic heritage. Galleria di Palazzo Zevallos Stigliano is a must-visit for art lovers, showcasing works from the Baroque period to contemporary pieces. For unique artisan goods, Galleria Prisco offers hand-painted ceramics, glass art, and local craftsmanship, all of which make for unforgettable souvenirs.

For a deeper dive into Neapolitan craftsmanship, Il Laboratorio della Ceramica offers ceramic-making workshops where visitors can watch artisans at work and even create their own pottery pieces. This provides an authentic experience that connects visitors to Naples' long tradition of artisan craftsmanship.

The unique boutiques and artisan shops in Naples are a reflection of the city's rich cultural heritage, offering everything from handmade ceramics and custom leather goods to traditional gold jewelry and artisanal food products. Whether you're seeking a bespoke fashion piece, a unique souvenir, or local delicacies, shopping in Naples provides an opportunity to connect with the heart of the city's craftsmanship and creativity. Exploring these hidden gems is a rewarding experience for any visitor looking to bring home a piece of Naples' vibrant culture.

EXPLORING VIA TOLEDO AND LOCAL MARKETS

Exploring Via Toledo and Local Markets is an essential experience for anyone visiting Naples, offering a vibrant mix of shopping, food, and authentic Neapolitan culture. Via Toledo is one of Naples' most iconic and bustling streets, lined with a variety of shops, boutiques, and historic sites, while the local markets add a sense of local life, with their colorful stalls and traditional goods.

- Via Toledo: The Heart of Shopping and City Life

Via Toledo is not only one of the main commercial streets in Naples but also a lively, historical artery that connects the Spanish Quarter to the Piazza del Plebiscito. The street is famous for its wide range of shops, including both international brands and local boutiques, making it a perfect spot for both window-shopping and serious retail therapy.

The street itself is a beautiful blend of history and modernity. As you walk down Via Toledo, you'll pass stunning historic buildings, including the

Galleria Umberto I, a magnificent glass-roofed shopping arcade with its elegant architecture and high-end boutiques. The Galleria is a perfect place to enjoy a coffee while admiring the intricate details of the space.

Along Via Toledo, you'll find designer fashion stores, shoe boutiques, and local artisans selling traditional wares, from ceramics to leather goods. The street is also home to numerous bookstores and art galleries, offering a glimpse into Naples' literary and artistic life. Whether you're looking for high-end fashion or unique, locally crafted goods, Via Toledo offers something for everyone.

In addition to shopping, Via Toledo is a great place to explore the vibrant Neapolitan street culture. The sidewalks are often filled with street performers, musicians, and artists, creating an exciting and lively atmosphere.

- Local Markets: A Taste of Authentic Naples

Naples is also known for its local markets, where you can experience the true spirit of the city. These markets are an integral part of daily life for Neapolitans, offering everything from fresh produce to traditional street food and handmade goods. Visiting the markets gives you a chance to experience the local culture up close and interact with the friendly and passionate vendors.

Mercato di Porta Nolana is one of Naples' most famous markets, offering a huge variety of fresh seafood, meats, cheese, and vegetables. Here, you can find the catch of the day, including squid, anchovies, and clams, all freshly prepared for cooking. The market is a great place to sample Neapolitan culinary traditions, like seafood pasta or fried fish from nearby food stalls.

Another popular market is Mercato di Pignasecca, the oldest in the city, known for its vibrant atmosphere and huge range of products. This market offers everything from fruits and vegetables to fresh pasta and spices, giving you a taste of Naples' rich culinary culture. Don't miss out on sampling some of the local street food from the stalls, such as pizza margherita, sfogliatella (a traditional pastry), or frittatina (fried pasta croquettes).

For those interested in handmade goods, the Mercato delle Pulci (flea market) in the Spaccanapoli area is a fascinating place to explore. Here, you can find antique furniture, vintage items, crafts, and ceramics, all with a distinct Neapolitan flair. It's an ideal spot for finding unique souvenirs or gifts.

The Vico dei Maiolicari street, located near the historic center, is another must-see for lovers of traditional Neapolitan ceramics. The shops here sell beautifully crafted hand-painted pottery, which makes for a perfect keepsake from your visit to Naples.

- The Vibrancy of Local Food Markets

Naples is renowned for its rich culinary culture, and the local markets are the perfect place to immerse yourself in the food scene. The Pignasecca Market is particularly famous for its street food vendors, offering a taste of authentic Neapolitan flavors. Pizza margherita is a must-try, often served from small stalls or pizzerias near the market. The combination of fresh, simple ingredients—tomato, mozzarella, and basil—make it a delicious and quintessentially Neapolitan experience.

Another iconic food experience is sampling sfogliatella, a flaky, sweet pastry filled with ricotta cheese and candied fruit, which can be found at bakeries and food stalls across the city. You can also try frittata di pasta, a savory dish made from leftover pasta mixed with eggs, cheese, and other ingredients, then fried into a crispy, golden snack.

For those who appreciate Italian wines, many of the markets sell locally produced Lacryma Christi, Greco di Tufo, and Fiano wines, which are perfect for pairing with any meal or enjoying by themselves.

- Walking Tours and Market Discoveries

Exploring Via Toledo and the nearby markets can be done at your own pace, but joining a walking tour can enhance the experience. Many local guides offer food tours or shopping tours of the historic center, where you'll learn about the history of the area, discover hidden gems, and sample local treats along the way. A food-focused walking tour may include stops at markets, bakeries, and local eateries, allowing you to taste traditional dishes and learn about their significance in Neapolitan culture.

Exploring Via Toledo and the local markets of Naples provides an authentic and enriching experience for anyone visiting the city. Whether you're interested in shopping for handmade goods and luxury fashion, discovering local street food, or simply immersing yourself in the vibrant atmosphere of Naples, these areas offer a true taste of the city's lively culture. With a mix of traditional crafts, fresh food, and lively street life, Via Toledo and the surrounding markets capture the essence of Neapolitan life.

SOUVENIRS AND MUST-HAVE KEEPSHAKES

Souvenirs and Must-Have Keepsakes from Naples capture the essence of the city's rich history, culture, and craftsmanship. Whether you're looking for a small token to remember your trip or a more substantial item, Naples offers a variety of unique and meaningful keepsakes that reflect its vibrant heritage. From handcrafted goods to delicious treats, here are some must-have souvenirs to bring home from Naples.

- Traditional Neapolitan Ceramics

One of the most iconic souvenirs from Naples is its ceramics. The city is famous for its hand-painted pottery, with intricate designs featuring bright colors and traditional motifs. Neapolitan ceramics are often inspired by the sea, nature, and local life, making them a beautiful reminder of the region's artistic traditions.

The Vico dei Maiolicari street is lined with artisan ceramic shops, where you can find plates, bowls, vases, and tiles decorated in the traditional blue and yellow or red and green patterns. Many of these pieces are hand-painted, ensuring that each item is unique. For something truly special, consider buying handmade tiles or a decorative majolica plate, which can be displayed at home as a piece of Neapolitan history.

- Cameos and Jewelry

Naples has a long tradition of goldsmithing and cameo carving, and the city is renowned for its cameo jewelry. Cameos are intricately carved portraits or scenes, typically made from shells, coral, or stone, and are often set in gold or silver.

You can find beautiful cameo necklaces, brooches, earrings, and rings at jewelry shops around the historic center, particularly on Via San Gregorio Armeno, known for its traditional craftwork. These pieces are not just jewelry but miniature works of art, with each one telling a story through its design. Cameo jewelry makes for a timeless and elegant souvenir, embodying the craftsmanship and history of Naples.

- Limoncello and Local Liquors

No visit to Naples would be complete without a bottle of Limoncello, the famous lemon liqueur from the Amalfi Coast. Limoncello is made from the zest of local lemons, which are renowned for their intense flavor and fragrance. This bright yellow drink is a perfect souvenir, as it reflects the essence of southern Italy's sunny, citrus-filled landscape.

You can find Limoncello in shops across Naples, often sold in decorative bottles. For a truly authentic experience, look for small-batch producers offering handcrafted Limoncello. Additionally, other regional liquors like Rucolino (a local herb liqueur) or Finocchietto (an anise-based drink) also make great gifts for those who enjoy trying new flavors.

- Neapolitan Pizza Stones and Accessories

Given Naples' status as the birthplace of pizza, a pizza-themed souvenir is a must. Look for pizza stones, pizzaiolo hats, and other pizza-making accessories that will help you recreate a piece of Naples at home. Some shops sell miniature pizza ovens or stone baking slabs, which can be used to bake authentic Neapolitan-style pizzas.

In addition to pizza accessories, you might also find ceramic pizza plates with colorful traditional designs, perfect for serving your homemade pizza in true Neapolitan style. These items make great souvenirs for food lovers and anyone who enjoys cooking at home.

- Traditional Neapolitan Street Food Snacks

Neapolitan street food is an essential part of the city's culinary culture, and bringing home some edible souvenirs can help you recreate the flavors of Naples at home. Popular items to bring back include:

- Limoncello-flavored sweets or candies, which are often sold in decorative tins or boxes.
- Neapolitan pastries, such as sfogliatella (a flaky pastry filled with ricotta and semolina) or pastiera (a sweet ricotta pie), which can be found in specialty shops. While the fresh

versions are best enjoyed locally, some shops sell packaged versions for travelers.
➢ Pasta in various shapes and sizes, including scialatielli (a local, thick pasta), which you can bring home and cook yourself for an authentic taste of Naples.

● Local Art and Paintings

Naples is home to a thriving art scene, and you'll find many small art galleries and craft shops offering works by local artists. These can range from paintings depicting scenes of Naples' vibrant life to handcrafted sculptures and prints. A piece of local art is a great way to capture the beauty of Naples' landscapes, historic sites, or everyday life.

For a more unique souvenir, you can also purchase a hand-painted tile or a small mosaic that reflects Naples' artistic traditions. These are perfect for decorating your home with a piece of the city's cultural heritage.

- Neapolitan Marquetry and Wood Crafts

Naples is famous for its marquetry, a delicate form of woodworking that creates intricate, detailed designs using wood inlays. These beautiful pieces often feature scenes of Italian landscapes, floral patterns, or historic landmarks. You can find marquetry boxes, trays, mirrors, and furniture at various artisan shops in Naples. These items are perfect for those looking for a sophisticated and practical souvenir that reflects the artistry of the region.

- Neapolitan Nativity Scenes (Presepi)

Another unique and deeply rooted tradition in Naples is the creation of Presepi, or Neapolitan nativity scenes. These intricate dioramas, which depict the birth of Jesus, are an iconic symbol of Naples. The Via San Gregorio Armeno street is a famous destination for purchasing these handmade nativity scenes, where you can find everything from traditional, classical scenes to more modern, humorous representations.

Presepi are typically made from clay, wood, and straw, with highly detailed figures of shepherds, angels, and farmers, each representing a part of Neapolitan life. Many shops along the street offer customized figures, so you can create a personalized nativity scene as a lasting keepsake.

When visiting Naples, you'll find a wide variety of souvenirs and keepsakes that capture the city's rich cultural heritage and craftsmanship. From handcrafted ceramics and cameo jewelry to Limoncello and Neapolitan pastries, the souvenirs you take home from Naples will serve as lasting reminders of your time in this vibrant and historic city. Whether you're looking for something to display at home, a delicious treat, or a piece of local art, Naples offers countless ways to bring a piece of its magic home with you.

CHAPTER EIGHT

NATURE AND OUTDOOR ADVENTURES

MOUNT VESUVIUS

Mount Vesuvius is one of the most famous and active volcanoes in the world, located near the city of Naples in southern Italy. It is particularly renowned for its catastrophic eruption in 79 AD, which destroyed the Roman cities of Pompeii and Herculaneum, leaving a rich archaeological legacy and offering insight into ancient Roman life.

Mount Vesuvius is a stratovolcano, formed by layers of hardened lava, ash, and other volcanic debris. Its eruptions have been both violent and highly destructive, with the 79 AD eruption being its most famous. This eruption buried the ancient cities of Pompeii and Herculaneum under meters of volcanic ash and pumice, preserving the cities and their inhabitants in a unique snapshot of daily life at the time.

The volcano has had several eruptions since, and although it has been dormant for long periods, it is closely monitored due to its potential for future activity. The last eruption occurred in 1944, and scientists continue to study the volcano to predict and understand its behavior.

Mount Vesuvius is one of the most popular attractions near Naples and offers visitors the chance to experience its immense power up close. There are several ways to visit the volcano and enjoy its views, hiking trails, and surrounding areas.

The most popular way to explore Mount Vesuvius is by hiking to the summit. The volcano's hiking trail is accessible and well-marked, taking visitors through volcanic terrain filled with rocky paths and dramatic views of the Bay of Naples, Pompeii, and the surrounding towns. The walk to the summit takes about 30 to 40 minutes and offers an incredible panoramic view of the area. At the top, visitors can peer into the volcano's crater, which is still an active geological feature. The edge of the crater provides a sense of the power that once erupted from within the mountain. On a clear day, the vistas are spectacular, and visitors can see Naples, the Amalfi Coast, and Pompeii in the distance.

Mount Vesuvius is also a part of the Vesuvius National Park, which encompasses the area around the volcano, offering lush landscapes, forests, and diverse flora and fauna. The park has several hiking trails that allow visitors to explore the slopes of the volcano and its unique ecosystems. In addition to hiking, the park is great for nature lovers who want to enjoy birdwatching and experience the natural beauty of the volcanic landscape.

For those interested in the scientific aspects of the volcano, the Vesuvius Observatory is an excellent spot to visit. Established in the 19th century, it is one of the oldest volcanic observatories in the world. Located near the summit, it has played a crucial role in monitoring the volcano's activity. The observatory offers informative exhibits about volcanic eruptions, the history of Mount Vesuvius, and the ongoing research into predicting eruptions. It is a valuable resource for understanding the science behind this active volcano.

A visit to Mount Vesuvius is often combined with trips to the nearby archaeological sites of Pompeii and Herculaneum. These ancient cities were buried under ash during the 79 AD eruption, and today they offer a fascinating glimpse into daily Roman life. Pompeii, the larger of the two sites, attracts millions of visitors each year. Visitors can walk through the streets, exploring the ruins of homes, baths, temples, and shops.

The preservation of Pompeii gives a vivid picture of ancient Roman life, with frescoes, mosaics, and even the remains of the city's inhabitants who were caught in the eruption. Herculaneum, while smaller and less crowded, is exceptionally well-preserved, with buildings, frescoes, and even wooden structures that provide a unique look at Roman domestic life.

Mount Vesuvius is easily accessible from Naples. Visitors can reach the base of the volcano by car, public transport, or via shuttle buses from nearby cities like Pompeii and Herculaneum. The summit of Mount Vesuvius is open year-round, but it's best to visit in spring or fall when the weather is milder for hiking. Summer can be very hot, so it's recommended to go early in the morning or later in the day to avoid the heat. Comfortable hiking shoes are essential, as the trail can be rocky and uneven. Bring plenty of water, sunscreen, and a hat to protect from the sun, especially if you're hiking in the summer months.

Mount Vesuvius is not just an active volcano but a symbol of the power of nature and the resilience of human history. It is a must-visit for anyone traveling to Naples, offering the chance to hike to the summit and peer into the crater, visit the nearby archaeological sites of Pompeii and Herculaneum, and learn about the scientific study of volcanology at the Vesuvius Observatory. Whether you're interested in geology, history, or simply breathtaking views, Mount Vesuvius provides an unforgettable experience.

NAPLES BAY AND THE AMALFI COAST

Naples Bay and the Amalfi Coast are two of Italy's most breathtakingly beautiful regions, offering an extraordinary blend of scenic landscapes, rich history, and charming coastal towns. Both are located in the Campania region, with Naples Bay serving as the gateway to the area, and the Amalfi Coast stretching along the southern edge of the Sorrentine Peninsula.

Naples Bay, or the Gulf of Naples, is a striking natural harbor surrounded by dramatic cliffs and the iconic Mount Vesuvius. It is home to the vibrant city of Naples, known for its rich history and culture. The bay itself is dotted with picturesque islands, such as Capri, Ischia, and Procida, each offering its own unique attractions and charm. Visitors can explore these islands by boat, enjoying the crystal-clear waters, scenic beauty, and tranquil atmosphere that each one offers. Capri, for example, is famous for its dramatic cliffs, luxury boutiques, and the enchanting Blue Grotto, while Ischia is known for its therapeutic thermal spas, and Procida provides a quieter, more laid-back experience with its colorful homes and charming streets.

The Amalfi Coast is a UNESCO World Heritage site, renowned for its steep cliffs, dramatic landscapes, and quaint villages that cling to the coastline. Stretching from Positano to Salerno, the Amalfi Coast is one of the most picturesque regions in the world. Positano, with its pastel-colored houses cascading down the cliffs, is perhaps the most famous town, offering narrow streets lined with shops, cafes, and art galleries. Amalfi, the historic heart of the coast, is home to the impressive Amalfi Cathedral and boasts beautiful beaches. Ravello, perched high above the coast, offers stunning views of the sea and is known for its magnificent villas and gardens, such as Villa Rufolo and Villa Cimbrone.

The Amalfi Coast is perfect for those who love outdoor activities. Hiking trails, such as the Path of the Gods, offer spectacular views of the coastline, while boat tours allow visitors to see the dramatic cliffs and hidden coves from the water. Kayaking, sailing, and swimming in the

Mediterranean are also popular activities. The area is famous for its lemons, particularly the Sfusato Amalfitano variety, and visitors can enjoy local lemon liqueur, limoncello, or indulge in fresh seafood dishes.

For those traveling to Naples Bay and the Amalfi Coast, spring and fall are the best times to visit. The weather is mild, and the crowds are smaller compared to the busy summer months. The region can be explored by car, public transportation, or by boat, with many towns offering ferry services between coastal destinations. Whether you're exploring the historic city of Naples, relaxing on the Amalfi Coast, or visiting the nearby islands, Naples Bay and the Amalfi Coast offer an unforgettable experience of Italy's coastal beauty, history, and culture.

DAY TRIPS TO CAPRI, ISCHIA, AND PROCIDA

Day trips to the islands of Capri, Ischia, and Procida are among the most memorable experiences when visiting Naples Bay. Each island offers its own unique charm, natural beauty, and historical significance, making them perfect destinations for a day of exploration and relaxation.

Capri is the most famous of the three islands, known for its dramatic cliffs, glamorous atmosphere, and stunning vistas. Located just a short ferry ride from Naples, Capri is a must-visit destination for anyone in the region. The island is divided into two main areas: the bustling town of Capri, perched on the hilltop, and the quieter village of Anacapri, located at a higher elevation. Visitors can take a funicular ride from the port to the main town, where they can wander through narrow streets lined with high-end boutiques, cafes, and art galleries. A boat tour around the island is highly recommended to see the famous Blue Grotto, a sea cave illuminated by a brilliant blue light, and other stunning natural landmarks like Faraglioni Rocks and the Marina Piccola.

For those seeking a more peaceful experience, a visit to Anacapri offers breathtaking views of the island and the surrounding sea. The Villa San Michele in Anacapri is a beautiful historic house with lush gardens and panoramic terraces. Another highlight of Capri is the Gardens of Augustus, where visitors can stroll through well-maintained gardens and enjoy one of the best views on the island, overlooking the Faraglioni Rocks and the bay.

Ischia, located to the west of Capri, is a larger island known for its thermal spas, lush green landscapes, and volcanic history. The island is famous for its therapeutic hot springs, and visitors can relax in one of the many spas or enjoy a soak in the natural thermal waters. Castello Aragonese, a medieval castle perched on a rocky islet connected to the main island by a bridge, is a must-see. Visitors can explore the castle's ancient walls, towers, and panoramic terraces, offering stunning views of the island and the surrounding sea.

Ischia's towns are also worth exploring. Forio, on the island's west coast, is home to beautiful beaches and a charming old town, while Sant'Angelo is a peaceful fishing village with colorful houses and picturesque streets. The island is known for its vineyards and olive groves, and visitors can enjoy local wines and traditional Italian cuisine in one of the many family-run restaurants.

Procida, the smallest of the three islands, offers a more laid-back and authentic experience compared to Capri and Ischia. This charming island is famous for its brightly colored buildings, narrow streets, and beautiful beaches. The main town, also called Procida, has a relaxed atmosphere, with cafes, local shops, and quiet waterfronts. The Marina di Corricella, a picturesque fishing village, is one of the island's most iconic spots, where visitors can enjoy fresh seafood and take in the stunning views of the harbor.

For those interested in history, Procida is home to several historic churches, including the Abbey of San Michele, and beautiful villas that offer a glimpse into the island's past. The island is also known for its role in literature and film, having served as the setting for books such as Elsa Morante's History and films like Il Postino.

Reaching the islands is easy from Naples, with frequent ferry services connecting the mainland to Capri, Ischia, and Procida. The ferries are a scenic way to travel, offering panoramic views of the Gulf of Naples as you approach each island.

Depending on the season, ferries can take anywhere from 30 minutes to an hour, making these islands perfect for a quick escape from the city.

Whether you're seeking the luxury and glamour of Capri, the relaxation and natural beauty of Ischia, or the authentic charm of Procida, each island provides a unique experience that can be enjoyed in a day.

PARKS AND GARDENS IN THE CITY

Naples is not only known for its rich history, vibrant culture, and stunning coastline, but it also boasts a variety of parks and gardens that offer peaceful retreats within the city. These green spaces provide visitors with a break from the hustle and bustle of urban life, while offering beautiful views, historic landscapes, and tranquil surroundings. Here are some of the top parks and gardens in Naples:

- Royal Palace of Naples Gardens (Giardini del Palazzo Reale)

Located in the heart of the city, the Royal Palace Gardens offer a serene escape with stunning views of the Gulf of Naples and the city. These beautifully landscaped gardens are attached to the historic Royal Palace of Naples, and their lush green areas are perfect for a leisurely stroll. The gardens feature a variety of trees, fountains, and sculptures, making it a lovely spot for visitors to relax and take in the surrounding views of the bay and Piazza del Plebiscito.

- Botanical Garden of Naples (Orto Botanico di Napoli)

The Botanical Garden of Naples is an extensive green space located in the historic center of the city. It spans over 12 hectares and is home to more than 2,000 species of plants from around the world. The garden was founded in the 18th century and is part of the University of Naples. Visitors can explore its wide range of plant collections, including tropical plants, medicinal herbs, and native species. The serene atmosphere and the wide variety of plant life make it an ideal place for nature lovers and those looking for a peaceful break from the city.

- Capodimonte Park (Parco di Capodimonte)

One of the largest green spaces in Naples, Capodimonte Park is located on a hilltop near the famous Capodimonte Museum. The park covers over 130 acres and offers panoramic views of the city and the Bay of Naples. It is a perfect spot for walking, jogging, or simply enjoying a picnic surrounded by nature. The park features centuries-old trees, well-maintained lawns, and several beautiful fountains. The Capodimonte Museum itself is also located within the park, making it easy to combine a visit to the museum with a relaxing stroll through the gardens.

- Villa Comunale (Public Villa)

The Villa Comunale, located along the seafront near the Lungomare promenade, is one of Naples' most popular public parks. The park offers lush lawns, palm trees, and stunning views of the Gulf of Naples. It's a popular spot for both locals and tourists, providing a peaceful place to relax or take a leisurely walk by the water. Visitors can enjoy the beautiful landscaping, including manicured flowerbeds, and sometimes take in a performance at the Pietro Tontodonati theater, located within the park.

- Virgiliano Park (Parco Virgiliano)

Situated on the Posillipo Hill, Virgiliano Park offers breathtaking panoramic views of the Gulf of Naples, the islands of Capri and Ischia, and Mount Vesuvius. The park is divided into several areas, each with its own charm, including walking paths, green lawns, and terraces with benches where visitors can take in the views. It is named after the Roman poet Virgil, who is believed to have lived in the area, and it is a perfect spot for those seeking a quiet place to relax while enjoying spectacular vistas.

- Mostra d'Oltremare Gardens

Located near the Fuorigrotta district, the Mostra d'Oltremare is an exhibition complex that also houses a lovely park with fountains, statues, and flowerbeds. The gardens are part of the fairgrounds that were originally designed for the 1940 International Exhibition. The park is well-maintained and provides a peaceful space for walking or resting. It's also home to the Naples Zoo, which adds to the attraction for families with children.

- Parco delle Rimembranze

Located near the historic Vomero district, Parco delle Rimembranze is a small, yet charming park that is popular for its calm atmosphere and scenic views over the city. The park features wide avenues lined with trees, perfect for an afternoon walk, and it's a quieter spot compared to some of the other larger parks in the city. The park is also home to several statues and memorials, adding to its historical charm.

- Park of the Royal Palace of Caserta (Reggia di Caserta)

While not technically within the city limits of Naples, the Royal Palace of Caserta and its surrounding gardens are easily accessible from the city and make for a wonderful day trip. The vast park surrounding the palace is one of the largest and most impressive royal gardens in Europe, featuring grand fountains, meticulously designed terraces, and sculptures. Visitors can explore the 120-hectare park, which includes lush green lawns, serene lakes, and forests, making it a fantastic place to spend a day surrounded by nature.

These parks and gardens offer a range of experiences for nature lovers, history enthusiasts, and anyone seeking a moment of peace amidst the urban excitement of Naples. Whether you're visiting a royal garden, wandering through botanical collections, or enjoying panoramic views of the Bay of Naples, these green spaces are the perfect way to immerse yourself in the natural beauty of the city.

CHAPTER NINE

NIGHTLIFE AND OUTDOOR ADVENTURES

BARS AND APERTIVO SPOTS

Naples is known for its vibrant nightlife and lively social scene, with bars and aperitivo spots offering a perfect place to relax and soak up the local atmosphere. Whether you're looking for a sophisticated cocktail lounge, a cozy neighborhood bar, or a lively café to enjoy a pre-dinner drink, Naples has plenty of options to satisfy all tastes. The tradition of aperitivo an early evening drink accompanied by small bites runs deep in the city's culture, and many of the city's bars and cafes are ideal spots to partake in this beloved ritual.

- Gran Caffè Gambrinus

Located in the heart of Naples, Gran Caffè Gambrinus is an iconic historic café that has been a favorite spot for locals and tourists alike for over a century. This elegant café is perfect for enjoying an aperitivo, with its classic Neapolitan atmosphere, ornate decor, and outdoor seating overlooking the lively Piazza del Plebiscito. Gran Caffè Gambrinus offers a wide selection of cocktails, including the famous Negroni and Spritz, paired with a delicious spread of appetizers. It's also a great spot to try a traditional sfogliatella, a local pastry, with your coffee or aperitivo.

- Caffè Mexico

Known for its historic reputation and traditional Neapolitan coffee, Caffè Mexico is also an excellent spot for aperitivo. Located in the Piazza Dante area, this café offers a cozy ambiance with a focus on high-quality drinks and local snacks. It's a great place to unwind with an Aperol Spritz or a Campari Soda, along with delicious taralli

(Italian snacks) and small sandwiches that accompany your drink.

- L'Antiquario

For those seeking a more intimate, upscale aperitivo experience, L'Antiquario in the Chiaia district is a stylish and elegant cocktail bar. With its vintage décor and expert mixologists, L'Antiquario offers a sophisticated take on the traditional aperitivo. The cocktail menu is creative, featuring unique twists on classic drinks, and the intimate atmosphere makes it a great choice for an evening out. The bartenders here take great pride in their craft, and you can expect expertly made cocktails alongside high-end appetizers such as marinated olives, cheeses, and cured meats.

- Vineria San Sebastiano

For wine lovers, Vineria San Sebastiano in the Spanish Quarter is a cozy wine bar that offers an impressive selection of local Campania wines.

This charming spot offers a rustic yet inviting atmosphere, perfect for enjoying a glass of wine with a plate of local cheeses or cured meats. The bar also serves a selection of traditional Italian aperitifs, such as Negronis and Spritz, alongside a variety of delicious small bites, making it ideal for a casual evening out with friends.

- Mimi Alla Ferrovia

Located near the Naples Central Train Station, Mimi Alla Ferrovia is a beloved bar and restaurant that specializes in a traditional Neapolitan aperitivo experience. Known for its hearty bites and local spirit, this spot is perfect for a laid-back, authentic aperitivo in a relaxed, bustling environment. It's a great place to try classic Neapolitan snacks, such as fried pizza or frittatine (fried pasta), while sipping on your favorite drink.

- Parthenope Caffè

For an aperitivo with a view, Parthenope Caffè offers a charming spot by the waterfront, with sweeping views of the Bay of Naples and Mount Vesuvius in the distance. Located along the Lungomare promenade, this café serves up refreshing cocktails like the Negroni Sbagliato or an Aperol Spritz, complemented by a selection of light bites such as bruschetta, olives, and mozzarella di bufala. It's the perfect place to enjoy a sunset drink while taking in the stunning views of the bay.

- Kestè

Located in the historic Spaccanapoli street, Kestè is a lively bar offering both great drinks and a lively social atmosphere. A popular spot for both locals and tourists, it features an extensive cocktail menu, including classics and creative concoctions. The bar also serves traditional Neapolitan aperitivo platters with a variety of cheeses, meats, and pizza bites, making it a great choice for those wanting to experience the true spirit of the city's aperitivo culture.

- Bar Nilo

For a more traditional experience, Bar Nilo in the Piazza Nilo area is a local favorite. Known for its strong coffee and classic Neapolitan cocktails, this small yet iconic bar has been serving locals for years. It's an excellent place to sip on an espresso or Caffè Napoletano, and it's also a good spot to try local liqueurs such as Limoncello or Strega. Bar Nilo is famous for its authentic atmosphere, complete with vintage decor and a welcoming vibe.

- La Stanza del Gusto

This stylish, modern bar located in the Vomero district offers a sophisticated take on the traditional Neapolitan aperitivo. La Stanza del Gusto features a creative menu with a wide range of cocktails, wines, and craft beers. The bar's minimalist yet elegant design creates an upscale atmosphere, perfect for sipping a well-crafted drink while indulging in gourmet appetizers, such as caprese skewers or mini arancini.

Whether you're looking for a classic café experience with a view of the Bay of Naples or a trendy bar serving artisanal cocktails, the city's bars and aperitivo spots offer something for everyone. In Naples, the tradition of aperitivo is more than just a pre-dinner drink; it's an experience that allows you to relax, socialize, and enjoy the city's lively atmosphere.

LIVE MUSIC AND JAZZ CLUBS

Naples boasts a lively music scene, with a variety of live music venues and jazz clubs offering everything from local talent to international performances. Whether you're a fan of jazz, blues, rock, or classical music, the city has a vibrant nightlife where you can enjoy live performances in intimate settings or larger venues. Here are some of the top spots in Naples to enjoy live music and jazz:

- Casa della Musica Federico I

A key venue for live music in Naples, Casa della Musica Federico I is known for hosting a diverse range of performances, including jazz, classical, and contemporary music. Located in the heart of the city, this venue offers an intimate setting for both emerging and established artists. The acoustics are excellent, and the performances are always engaging, making it a great spot for music lovers looking for a quality night out. It often hosts jazz concerts, classical recitals, and other live performances.

- Napoli Jazz Club

For a dedicated jazz experience, Napoli Jazz Club is a must-visit. Located in the Chiaia district, this cozy venue is one of the city's leading jazz spots, offering live performances almost every night. The club features both local and international jazz musicians, from traditional jazz to contemporary experimental sounds. The intimate atmosphere, combined with excellent acoustics, makes it a perfect place to enjoy high-quality jazz music in Naples. The club also serves drinks and light bites, enhancing the overall experience of enjoying a night out in the city.

- Blue Note Napoli

A branch of the iconic Blue Note jazz clubs found worldwide, Blue Note Napoli brings world-class jazz performances to the city. Located in the Vicoletto Belledonne area, this venue offers a sophisticated yet relaxed atmosphere with a focus on international jazz talent. With a modern, stylish interior and great acoustics, it's one of the best places in Naples to catch top-tier jazz performances. The club regularly hosts renowned jazz musicians and offers a mix of concerts, jam sessions, and themed nights.

- Arenile di Bagnoli

For those looking to enjoy live music in a more laid-back, beachside setting, Arenile di Bagnoli is a popular spot in the Bagnoli district of Naples. While it's known primarily as a venue for live rock and indie music, Arenile also hosts jazz performances from time to time, often in the form of jazz fusion or contemporary jazz. The venue is spacious, with an outdoor area that offers stunning views of the coast, making it a perfect place to enjoy live music with a relaxed atmosphere.

- Caffè degli Artisti

Located in the heart of Naples' historic center, Caffè degli Artisti is a charming café and live music venue known for its intimate, artistic vibe. The café often features live jazz performances, local bands, and acoustic sessions. The venue has a cozy, bohemian feel, with eclectic décor and a welcoming atmosphere, making it an ideal spot to enjoy a drink while listening to live music. It's a great place to catch up-and-coming local talent in a relaxed and comfortable environment.

- Flegrea Jazz Club

Located in the Fuorigrotta area of Naples, the Flegrea Jazz Club is a beloved venue for jazz lovers, featuring performances from some of the best local and international jazz musicians. The intimate setting allows for a close connection with the performers, making it a great place to experience jazz up close. The club is well-known for its commitment to preserving the tradition of jazz, while also promoting newer styles and artists. The atmosphere is warm and welcoming, and the club's cozy ambiance makes it a great spot to spend an evening immersed in great live music.

- Jungle Bar

For a more casual live music experience, Jungle Bar is a popular venue among locals. Situated in the Vomero district, this vibrant bar offers a mix of live music genres, including jazz, blues, and funk. The intimate setting and friendly atmosphere make it a great place to discover new bands and artists. Jungle Bar often hosts jam sessions and live performances, offering a great chance to hear a variety of musical styles in an informal and fun environment.

- Teatro San Carlo

While primarily known as the historic opera house of Naples, Teatro San Carlo also hosts a variety of live music performances, including classical concerts, orchestral performances, and occasionally jazz and contemporary music events. The venue itself is one of the most prestigious and beautiful in the world, offering an incredible cultural experience. For those interested in a more formal night out with live music, Teatro San Carlo offers an unforgettable setting.

- Vulcanico

For a unique experience, Vulcanico is an underground venue in Naples that features live jazz and other genres of music. Located in the Piazza Bellini area, this small, intimate venue has a warm, underground vibe and is known for its experimental music events and live jazz performances. It's a great place for those seeking a more underground, off-the-beaten-path music scene.

- Libreria Berisio

A hidden gem in Naples, Libreria Berisio is primarily a bookstore but also hosts live jazz performances. The intimate space, surrounded by books, creates a cozy setting for small jazz concerts, often featuring talented local musicians. It's a wonderful place for those who appreciate the fusion of culture, literature, and live music.

Naples offers a wide range of venues for live music and jazz lovers, from intimate clubs to larger concert halls, each offering something unique for music enthusiasts. Whether you want to experience traditional jazz, modern fusion, or a casual jam session, the city's vibrant music scene provides plenty of opportunities to enjoy top-notch live performances.

THEATERS AND CULTURAL EVENTS

Naples is a city with a rich cultural heritage, and its theaters and cultural events are a reflection of this vibrant artistic tradition. From opera and ballet to contemporary performances and festivals, Naples offers a wide range of theatrical and cultural experiences that will captivate both locals and visitors alike. Here are some of the most notable theaters and cultural events to explore in the city:

- Teatro di San Carlo

As one of the most prestigious opera houses in the world, Teatro di San Carlo is the crown jewel of Naples' cultural scene. Opened in 1737, this historic theater is renowned for its stunning architecture, including its lavish interiors and grand chandelier. It is home to a variety of performances, including opera, ballet, classical concerts, and special events. Attending a performance here is a must for any visitor who appreciates high art and the grandeur of Italian opera. The theater hosts a diverse range of performances throughout the year, featuring both internationally renowned artists and local talent.

- Teatro Mercadante

Another important cultural venue in Naples is the Teatro Mercadante, a prominent theater that dates back to the 19th century. Located in the historic center of the city, Teatro Mercadante hosts a wide variety of performances, including classical and contemporary theater, dance, and experimental productions. The venue is known for its modern interpretations of classic works as well as innovative performances that explore contemporary themes. It is a central hub for Naples' cultural life and is a must-visit for anyone interested in the local theater scene.

- Teatro Bellini

Located in the Piazza Bellini area, Teatro Bellini is one of the most beloved theaters in Naples. The venue is known for its diverse programming, which includes everything from classical opera and ballet to modern plays and experimental performances. Teatro Bellini is particularly renowned for its commitment to contemporary theater, with many of its productions pushing the boundaries of traditional performance styles. The theater's intimate setting allows for a close connection between the performers and the audience, making it a popular spot for both locals and visitors.

- Cultural Events and Festivals

In addition to its theaters, Naples hosts a variety of cultural events and festivals throughout the year, celebrating everything from classical music to local traditions and contemporary art. Here are some of the major cultural events to consider during your visit:

- Naples Theater Festival

The Naples Theater Festival is one of the city's most important cultural events, celebrating both Italian and international theater. Held annually, the festival brings together a wide range of performances, including classical and contemporary plays, dance performances, and more. It features some of the best Italian theater companies as well as international guests, creating a diverse and dynamic cultural atmosphere. The festival typically takes place during the summer months and takes place in various venues throughout the city, including the historic theaters and outdoor spaces.

- Festival di San Gennaro

The Festival di San Gennaro, held in honor of the city's patron saint, is one of Naples' most important religious and cultural events. It takes place each year in September and is marked by a series of religious processions, festivals, and cultural activities. The festival culminates in the famous miracle of the liquefaction of San Gennaro's blood, a phenomenon that is believed to be a sign of the saint's favor. This event is accompanied by music, performances, and street celebrations, giving visitors a chance to experience Naples' rich religious traditions and vibrant cultural life.

- Comicon (Naples Comic Con)

For fans of pop culture, comics, and animation, Comicon is a major cultural event held annually in Naples. This festival attracts thousands of visitors, featuring panels, workshops, cosplay contests, and exhibitions dedicated to comic books, video games, movies, and more. It's a celebration of creativity and fandom, and it brings together artists, creators, and fans from around the world. Held at the Mostra d'Oltremare, Comicon is a fun and lively event that adds a modern and international touch to Naples' cultural calendar.

- Naples Jazz Festival

Jazz lovers will appreciate the Naples Jazz Festival, an annual event that takes place in various venues across the city, including outdoor spaces, theaters, and jazz clubs. The festival features performances by renowned international jazz musicians, as well as local talent. It's a great opportunity to enjoy high-quality live music in the heart of Naples, with concerts ranging from classic jazz to modern fusion and experimental styles. The festival typically takes place in the summer months, attracting both seasoned jazz enthusiasts and newcomers to the genre.

- The Christmas Concerts and Festivals

During the Christmas season, Naples is filled with holiday-themed events, including concerts, theater productions, and street festivals. One of the most famous traditions is the Concerts of the Royal Palace, which takes place in the Royal Palace of Naples. The palace becomes a cultural hub during the holidays, hosting classical concerts, performances of Neapolitan music, and other festive events. Additionally, the streets of Naples come alive with holiday decorations, street markets, and performances, adding a magical atmosphere to the city during the Christmas season.

- Naples International Film Festival

For film enthusiasts, the Naples International Film Festival offers a chance to see the latest international films and meet filmmakers. This annual event takes place in the fall and showcases a wide range of films from across the globe, including documentaries, feature films, and shorts. The festival is a celebration of cinema, offering screenings, awards, and discussions with filmmakers. It's a fantastic opportunity for those interested in the art of filmmaking to explore the latest trends and innovations in the world of cinema.

- Teatro Nuovo and Contemporary Art

While not a traditional theater, the Teatro Nuovo is another key cultural venue in Naples, with a focus on contemporary performances and experimental theater. It regularly hosts avant-garde performances and is known for pushing the boundaries of conventional theater. Visitors interested in the intersection of theater, performance art, and contemporary cultural expressions will find Teatro Nuovo to be an exciting and thought-provoking venue.

Naples offers a wealth of theatrical and cultural experiences, whether you're looking for world-class opera in a historic venue, contemporary theater productions, or lively festivals celebrating local traditions. With its diverse cultural calendar, the city provides endless opportunities to explore the arts and immerse yourself in the cultural life of one of Italy's most vibrant cities.

CHAPTER TEN

DAY TRIPS AND EXCURSION

POMPEII AND HERCULANEUM

Pompeii and Herculaneum are two of the most significant archaeological sites in the world, offering a unique and remarkable glimpse into ancient Roman life. Both cities were destroyed and buried by the catastrophic eruption of Mount Vesuvius in AD 79, preserving them in a way that provides us with an unparalleled view of Roman urban life, art, and culture. Visiting these sites is like stepping back in time, offering a vivid and detailed understanding of how the Romans lived, worked, and interacted.

Pompeii is the larger and more famous of the two, attracting millions of visitors each year. The city was home to approximately 20,000 people at the time of its destruction. Pompeii was buried under a thick layer of volcanic ash and pumice, which helped preserve the city in remarkable detail. The excavation of Pompeii began in the 18th century and continues to this day, with ongoing discoveries that shed light on the daily lives of its residents. Walking through the streets of Pompeii feels like stepping into a time capsule, with buildings, frescoes, mosaics, and even human remains still intact. The site is vast, with over 66 hectares (163 acres) of the city exposed to visitors. You can explore the ancient streets, see the homes of the wealthy, visit public spaces, and witness the city's sophisticated urban planning.

Among the highlights of Pompeii are the Forum, which served as the central public square where political, religious, and social events took place; the Amphitheater, one of the oldest and best-preserved Roman amphitheaters, where gladiatorial games were held; and the House of the Faun, a grand residence known for its beautiful mosaics, including the famous "Alexander Mosaic" depicting the battle between Alexander the Great and Darius III. Other notable sites include the Villa of the Mysteries, which is famous for its series of mysterious frescoes believed to depict initiation rites or religious rituals. Additionally, Pompeii offers a chance to walk on original Roman streets, complete with stepping stones designed to help pedestrians cross flooded roads, providing an authentic experience of life in ancient Rome.

Herculaneum, while smaller and less well-known than Pompeii, is equally fascinating and offers a more intimate experience. It was a wealthier city and, unlike Pompeii, it was buried by a hot pyroclastic surge rather than ash. This means that many organic materials, such as wooden structures, furniture, and even food, were preserved in a remarkable state. The site is smaller, covering around 20 hectares (49 acres), but it offers extraordinary preservation, allowing visitors to see many aspects of ancient life that have not survived in other ancient cities.

The House of the Deer is one of the finest examples of a wealthy Herculaneum home, with stunning mosaics and frescoes that reflect the high status of its inhabitants. The House of the Mosaic Atrium is another beautiful residence known for its intricate mosaic floors depicting scenes from Greek mythology. The Palaestra, an ancient gymnasium, provides a glimpse into the physical culture of Herculaneum's residents, while the Boat Sheds offer an emotional and poignant insight into the final moments of the city's inhabitants. Excavations along the waterfront have revealed the remains of boats and those who perished trying to escape the eruption, offering a rare glimpse of the catastrophic event.

Visiting Herculaneum is often a quieter and more focused experience compared to Pompeii, thanks to its smaller size and fewer visitors. The preservation of organic materials, such as carbonized furniture and even food, offers a more personal and intimate look at ancient Roman life. It's possible to explore the entire site in just a few hours, which makes it ideal for visitors who want a less crowded and more contemplative experience.

Both Pompeii and Herculaneum are easily accessible from Naples. Pompeii is about a 30-minute train ride from the city, while Herculaneum is around 20 minutes away. Many visitors choose to explore both sites in one day, although taking time to appreciate each one over two days offers a more in-depth experience.

While Pompeii is larger and offers a broader scope of ancient Roman life with its bustling streets, forums, and public spaces, Herculaneum provides a more intimate experience with its well-preserved homes and organic materials that tell a more detailed story about the lives of the city's residents. Both sites are incredibly important for understanding the Roman world, and each offers something unique for visitors to discover.

Practical tips for visiting Pompeii and Herculaneum include wearing comfortable shoes due to the uneven terrain, bringing water, sunscreen, and a hat to protect yourself from the sun, and considering guided tours to enrich your experience. Both sites can be explored independently, but a knowledgeable guide can provide invaluable context and insight. For a more comprehensive experience, you can also combine your visit with a hike to the summit of Mount Vesuvius, the volcano responsible for the destruction of both cities. Visiting these ancient ruins allows you to connect with history in a profound way, making Pompeii and Herculaneum essential stops for anyone interested in the ancient world.

SORRENTO AND THE AMALFI COAST

Sorrento and the Amalfi Coast are two of Italy's most famous and picturesque destinations, offering breathtaking views, charming towns, rich history, and a unique Mediterranean atmosphere. These areas are ideal for travelers seeking beauty, culture, and relaxation, with their coastal villages, stunning landscapes, and countless activities to enjoy.

Sorrento is a scenic town perched above the Bay of Naples, offering magnificent views of the water and Mount Vesuvius in the distance. It is often considered the gateway to the Amalfi Coast, serving as a base for exploring the region. The town itself is filled with narrow, winding streets, quaint piazzas, and elegant villas. Piazza Tasso is the heart of Sorrento, surrounded by cafes, restaurants, and shops. Visitors can also explore the Cattedrale di Sorrento, a beautiful cathedral, and the Museo Correale di Terranova, which houses art collections and local historical exhibits. Sorrento is famous for its production of limoncello, a traditional lemon liqueur, and visitors can enjoy tasting it in local shops or at bars and restaurants. The town offers a relaxed vibe, with plenty of opportunities to stroll through its charming streets and enjoy its picturesque coastal views.

The Amalfi Coast itself is a UNESCO World Heritage site, stretching along the southern edge of the Sorrentine Peninsula. Known for its dramatic cliffs, crystal-clear waters, and quaint villages, the coast is one of the most scenic destinations in the world. Its narrow roads wind along steep hillsides, providing spectacular vistas of the Mediterranean. The coastal area is dotted with small towns and villages, each offering unique experiences, from the glamorous Positano to the quieter Ravello.

Positano is perhaps the most famous town along the Amalfi Coast, known for its colorful buildings that cascade down the hillside toward the sea. The town is perched on the cliffs, and visitors can explore its narrow streets filled with boutique shops, cafes, and art galleries. The beach below, while small, offers a perfect place to relax and enjoy the stunning views of the surrounding cliffs. Positano is also renowned for its restaurants, offering fresh seafood, traditional pasta dishes, and lemon-infused desserts. It is a popular destination for both daytime relaxation and evening nightlife, with many bars and restaurants offering sweeping views of the coast.

Amalfi, the town that gives the coast its name, is another highlight. Amalfi boasts a rich maritime history as a former powerful naval republic. The town is home to the striking Duomo di Amalfi, a cathedral that blends Arab-Norman and Byzantine architecture. The town's narrow streets are lined with cafes, shops, and historical buildings, offering a charming atmosphere for visitors to explore. Amalfi is also famous for its Amalfi paper, a centuries-old tradition of handcrafted paper. Visitors can find paper-making shops where they can see this unique craft being demonstrated.

Ravello, a town perched high above the coast, offers a more peaceful and less crowded experience. Known for its stunning gardens and villas, including Villa Rufolo and Villa Cimbrone, Ravello provides some of the best views on the Amalfi Coast. The Villa Rufolo is famous for its beautiful terraced gardens, while Villa Cimbrone offers panoramic vistas of the coast from its lofty position. Ravello is also home to the Ravello Festival, an annual music festival that attracts world-class performers and offers a unique cultural experience in an unforgettable setting.

Atrani and Praiano are two lesser-known but equally beautiful towns on the Amalfi Coast.

Atrani, located just below Amalfi, is a quiet, charming village with narrow streets and stunning coastal views. Its tranquil atmosphere and local cafes make it an excellent place to experience authentic Italian village life. Praiano, situated between Positano and Amalfi, is a peaceful retreat with scenic beaches, crystal-clear waters, and charming streets. It's the perfect destination for those looking to escape the crowds and enjoy the beauty of the coast in a quieter setting.

Capri, the famous island off the coast of Sorrento, is another must-visit destination. Known for its dramatic cliffs, crystal-clear waters, and luxury atmosphere, Capri attracts visitors from around the world. The island is famous for its Blue Grotto, a sea cave illuminated by an otherworldly blue light, and visitors can take boat tours to explore this natural wonder. Anacapri, a smaller town on the island, offers stunning views and the chance to take a chairlift up to Mount Solaro for panoramic vistas. Capri's charming streets are lined with luxury boutiques, cafes, and restaurants, making it a perfect destination for those seeking a glamorous getaway.

Exploring the Amalfi Coast is often best done by car, as the narrow and winding roads offer the most spectacular views. However, driving can be challenging, especially during the high season when the roads can be crowded with tourists. For a more relaxing experience, many travelers opt for boat tours, which allow them to view the coastline from the sea and explore hidden beaches and coves that are inaccessible by land.

For those who enjoy outdoor activities, the Amalfi Coast offers plenty of options. Hiking enthusiasts can take on the Path of the Gods (Sentiero degli Dei), a scenic trail that offers panoramic views of the coastline, lush forests, and remote villages. The coast is also perfect for swimming, snorkeling, and kayaking in its crystal-clear waters. Visitors can take guided tours to explore the area's ancient ruins, including Pompeii and Herculaneum, or visit the Villa Jovis on Capri for a historical experience.

The best time to visit Sorrento and the Amalfi Coast is during the spring and autumn months (April to June and September to October). During these seasons, the weather is pleasant, and the crowds are smaller, allowing for a more relaxed experience. The summer months can be hot and crowded, so it's advisable to book accommodations and activities well in advance if visiting during this time. Winter offers a quieter experience, although some attractions may be closed, and the weather can be cooler.

Sorrento and the Amalfi Coast offer a unique blend of natural beauty, cultural heritage, and Mediterranean charm. Whether you're exploring the lively streets of Positano, relaxing on the beaches of Amalfi, or taking in the serene views from Ravello, these destinations are sure to leave a lasting impression. With their stunning landscapes, rich history, and vibrant local culture, Sorrento and the Amalfi Coast provide the perfect setting for an unforgettable Italian escape.

EXPLORING CASERTA AND ITS ROYAL PALACE

Caserta, a charming city located in the Campania region of southern Italy, is best known for its stunning Royal Palace of Caserta (Reggia di Caserta), one of the largest and most magnificent royal residences in Europe. The city, with its rich history and impressive architectural landmarks, offers a unique glimpse into Italy's royal past and is a must-visit destination for those exploring the area.

- The Royal Palace of Caserta

The crown jewel of Caserta is undoubtedly the Royal Palace, a UNESCO World Heritage site renowned for its grandeur and architectural beauty. Commissioned by King Charles VII of Naples in the 18th century, the palace was designed by the architect Luigi Vanvitelli and modeled after the famous Palace of Versailles in France. It was constructed as the residence of the Bourbon kings of Naples and served as their royal seat for over a century.

The palace is an architectural masterpiece, with over 1,200 rooms, including grand halls, opulent chambers, and impressive state apartments. The Palazzo Reale, with its beautiful neoclassical facades, is a striking example of Baroque and Rococo architecture. Visitors can explore its majestic rooms, including the Royal Apartments, the Throne Room, and the Hall of Mirrors, which showcase the luxurious lifestyle of the Bourbon court. The interior of the palace is adorned with exquisite frescoes, elaborate chandeliers, and elegant furnishings, offering a glimpse into the past grandeur of the royal family.

One of the most striking features of the palace is its extensive gardens, which are among the largest in Europe. The gardens stretch for over three kilometers and are divided into several sections, including formal French-style gardens, English-style landscapes, and lush, forested areas. The Great Waterfall, located at the end of the gardens, is a spectacular sight, with water cascading down a series of fountains and reflecting pools, creating a dramatic visual effect. The gardens are perfect for leisurely walks, offering visitors a peaceful escape while enjoying beautiful views of the surrounding countryside.

- Visiting the Royal Palace

A visit to the Royal Palace of Caserta is a journey through Italian history and architecture. The palace is open to the public and offers a variety of guided tours that provide detailed insights into the palace's history, its former royal inhabitants, and the artistic treasures housed within. The expansive gardens are also open for exploration, and visitors can take a leisurely stroll through the grounds, visit the fountains, or relax by the serene ponds.

The Royal Palace is well connected to the city center and can be easily reached by public transport, car, or walking. The palace is open year-round, although it's recommended to visit during the spring or autumn months when the weather is pleasant, and the gardens are in full bloom.

- Exploring the City of Caserta

While the Royal Palace is the main attraction, Caserta itself has much to offer. The city has a rich history dating back to Roman times, and visitors can explore its charming streets, local markets, and historical sites. The Cathedral of San Michele Arcangelo, a beautiful Baroque church located in the heart of Caserta, is a significant religious and architectural landmark in the city. It features a stunning facade and ornate interior, making it a peaceful place to visit after exploring the busy streets.

Caserta is also home to several other historic buildings, including the Palazzo Ducale, a former ducal palace, and the Aqueduct of Vanvitelli, an impressive 18th-century aqueduct that was built to bring water to the Royal Palace. The aqueduct stretches for over 38 kilometers and is a remarkable feat of engineering.

For those interested in local cuisine, Caserta offers a variety of traditional dishes. The city is known for its mozzarella di bufala, a delicious buffalo mozzarella cheese that is produced in the surrounding countryside. Visitors can visit local dairies to learn about the cheese-making process and sample this creamy, fresh delicacy. Additionally, Caserta boasts several charming cafes and restaurants, where visitors can enjoy authentic Italian dishes, including pasta, pizza, and desserts.

- Day Trips from Caserta

Caserta is well-located for exploring other nearby attractions. The ancient Roman city of Pompeii, with its fascinating archaeological sites, is just a short drive away. Visitors can walk through the preserved streets of Pompeii, visit the ancient homes, temples, and baths, and learn about life in the Roman Empire before the eruption of Mount Vesuvius in 79 AD.

For those interested in nature, the National Park of the Casertan Forest offers a peaceful retreat into the lush hills and woodlands surrounding Caserta. The park features numerous trails for hiking, cycling, and enjoying the outdoors, and is home to a variety of flora and fauna. Additionally, the city's proximity to Naples and the Amalfi Coast makes it an ideal starting point for day trips to the region's famous coastal towns and historic sites.

Caserta, with its majestic Royal Palace, historical landmarks, and beautiful landscapes, is a captivating destination that offers a unique glimpse into Italy's royal past. Whether you're admiring the opulence of the Royal Palace, wandering through its expansive gardens, or exploring the city's charming streets, Caserta promises an unforgettable experience. The combination of history, architecture, and natural beauty makes it a must-see destination for travelers visiting southern Italy.

WINERY TOURS IN CAMPANIA

Winery tours in Campania offer an unforgettable experience for wine lovers, blending the region's natural beauty with a deep-rooted winemaking tradition. Located in southern Italy, Campania is known for its volcanic soils, Mediterranean climate, and a rich history of grape cultivation that stretches back thousands of years. The region is home to some of the most distinctive wines in

Italy, made from unique, local grape varieties that flourish in the fertile hillsides and volcanic landscapes.

The three main wine regions of Campania – Irpinia, the Sorrentine Peninsula, and the area around Mount Vesuvius – are where the most notable wines are produced. Irpinia, with its cool climate and mountainous terrain, is known for producing some of the region's finest white wines, including Fiano di Avellino and Greco di Tufo, as well as the red Taurasi. The Sorrentine Peninsula, near Naples, is famed for Lacryma Christi, a wine that reflects the area's coastal influences, made from local grapes such as Piedirosso and Coda di Volpe. Mount Vesuvius, with its volcanic slopes, produces distinctive wines that carry the earthy, mineral qualities of the region's volcanic soil, including Vesuvio wine made from the Caprettone grape.

A visit to Campania's wineries allows guests to experience not only the fine wines but also the stunning landscapes and the winemaking process that has been passed down through generations. Many of the wineries in Campania offer guided tours that take visitors through their vineyards, explaining the history of their vineyards, the varieties of grapes grown, and the meticulous methods used to produce their wines. These tours often include a walk through the vineyards, where guests can admire the panoramic views of the rolling hills, coastal landscapes, or the dramatic slopes of Mount Vesuvius, before heading to the cellars to learn about the fermentation and aging processes.

The wine tastings that follow are the highlight of any winery visit. Guests are typically treated to a selection of the winery's finest wines, often accompanied by local specialties like mozzarella di bufala, cured meats, fresh bread, and local cheeses. Some wineries even offer more elaborate food pairings, with multi-course meals that pair perfectly with the wines, allowing visitors to fully appreciate how Campania's wines complement its cuisine. Whether it's a crisp and aromatic Fiano di Avellino, a complex Taurasi, or the fresh, zesty Lacryma Christi, each wine is a reflection of the region's unique terroir and winemaking heritage.

One of the most enriching aspects of these tours is the opportunity to meet the winemakers themselves. Many of the wineries are family-owned and run, and the passionate winemakers often lead the tours, sharing their personal stories and insights into the winemaking process. They offer a deeper understanding of the challenges they face, the traditions they uphold, and the innovations they're introducing to modern winemaking. Visitors have the chance to ask questions, learn about the history of the wines, and hear about the impact of local traditions and the region's natural environment on the final product.

Some of the top wineries to visit in Campania include Mastroberardino, one of the oldest and most prestigious wineries in Irpinia, known for its exceptional Fiano di Avellino and Taurasi wines. Feudi di San Gregorio, also in Irpinia, is another renowned winery that offers modern facilities and high-quality wines, offering visitors a chance to taste some of the region's best wines while enjoying panoramic views of the vineyards. Cantine dell'Angelo, located on the slopes of Mount Vesuvius, is a family-run winery that specializes in wines made from local grapes grown in volcanic soils, producing unique and flavorful wines such as Vesuvio. Lacryma Christi di Vesuvio, a winery situated near Naples, is famous for its production of Lacryma Christi, a wine that reflects the region's volcanic terroir.

For those looking to explore the region in the harvest season (late summer to early autumn), there is no better time to visit. It's a time when the vineyards are buzzing with activity, and the grapes are ready to be picked. However, tours are available throughout the year, with spring and autumn offering mild weather and fewer crowds. Even in winter, the wineries remain open, providing an intimate experience for those who prefer a quieter, more personal tour.

Campania's winery tours not only offer an opportunity to taste some of the finest wines but also give guests a deeper understanding of the region's rich agricultural heritage and its important role in Italy's winemaking tradition. Whether you're wandering through the lush vineyards, learning about the history and techniques behind each bottle, or savoring wines paired with regional delicacies, a winery tour in Campania is an enriching and memorable experience.

CHAPTER ELEVEN

PRACTICAL TIPS FOR TRAVELERS

HEALTH AND SAFETY IN NAPLES

When visiting Naples, health and safety should be a priority to ensure a smooth and enjoyable trip. Like many major cities, Naples presents some general considerations, but it remains a welcoming and vibrant destination for tourists. Here's an overview of health and safety tips for visitors to Naples.

- Health and Medical Care

Naples, like other parts of Italy, has a well-established healthcare system, and there are numerous hospitals, clinics, and pharmacies across the city. Visitors can expect a high standard of medical care in emergencies.

1. Pharmacies: Pharmacies in Naples are widely available, and they often have extended hours, with some open late or even 24 hours. Many pharmacy staff members speak English, and they can assist with over-the-counter medications or offer advice on basic health concerns. It's also a good idea to have a list of any prescription medications you may need while traveling.

2. Hospitals and Clinics: There are several hospitals in Naples, including Ospedale Cardarelli, one of the largest and most important hospitals in the region. In an emergency, you can dial 112 (the European emergency number) for ambulance services, and they will respond promptly.

3. Travel Insurance: It's advisable to have comprehensive travel insurance that includes medical coverage in case of illness or accidents. Ensure that the policy covers

medical evacuations, as some situations may require air travel for more specialized care.

4. Vaccinations and Health Precautions: Make sure you're up to date with any necessary vaccinations, especially if you're traveling from outside the EU. There are no mandatory vaccinations for traveling to Italy, but some basic precautions regarding food and water hygiene are always recommended, especially for those with sensitive stomachs. Drink bottled water if you're concerned about the tap water, although it is generally safe to drink in Naples.

- Safety Concerns

Naples, while generally safe for tourists, does have areas where caution should be exercised. However, many of the most visited spots, including the historic center, the waterfront, and major tourist attractions, are safe to explore.

1. Pickpocketing and Theft: Like in many large cities, pickpocketing is common in crowded areas, especially in tourist-heavy zones such as Spaccanapoli, Piazza del Plebiscito, and on public transport. Always keep an eye on your belongings, especially in busy spots. Use a money belt, keep your valuables in front pockets, and avoid carrying too much cash or expensive electronics in plain sight.

2. Street Scams: Be aware of common scams targeting tourists. These can include individuals asking for donations, offering unsolicited "friendship bracelets," or trying to sell fake tickets or goods. Politely refuse any unsolicited offers and avoid engaging with scam artists.

3. Public Transport Safety: Public transportation in Naples, including buses and the metro, is generally safe. However, be cautious during rush hours when trains and

buses can become crowded. Keep your belongings close, especially when traveling on the Linea 1 metro or the funiculars, where pickpockets may operate.

4. Walking at Night: While Naples is generally safe at night, some areas—especially the outskirts and certain neighborhoods like Scampia and Secondigliano—are best avoided after dark due to higher crime rates. Stick to well-lit, central areas such as the historic center and along the waterfront when walking at night.

5. Traffic and Road Safety: Naples is known for its chaotic driving conditions, with aggressive drivers, scooters weaving in and out of traffic, and often limited parking. Be careful when crossing streets, even at pedestrian crossings, and always look both ways before stepping onto the road. If you're renting a car, familiarize yourself with the

local traffic rules and be prepared for the bustling streets.

6. Emergency Numbers: In the event of an emergency, the general European emergency number is 112. For police-related emergencies, you can also dial 113, and for medical emergencies, 118 is the dedicated ambulance number.

● Natural Hazards and Environmental Factors
Naples sits near Mount Vesuvius, one of the most famous active volcanoes in the world. While the likelihood of a volcanic eruption during your visit is very low, it's important to be aware of evacuation routes and safety measures, particularly if you plan to visit the Vesuvius National Park. It's also worth checking for any specific volcanic alerts or advisories before traveling to the area.

In addition, Naples' climate is Mediterranean, with hot summers and mild winters. During the summer months, heat waves can occur, and it's important to stay hydrated, wear sunscreen, and avoid long periods of direct sun exposure, especially in the afternoon. If you're planning outdoor activities, wear light, breathable clothing and sturdy footwear.

- Food and Water Safety

The food in Naples is a highlight for many visitors, but it's important to follow some basic food safety guidelines:

1. Tap water: Tap water is generally safe to drink in Naples, but if you have concerns, bottled water is widely available.
2. Street Food: While Naples is famous for its pizza and street food, always choose vendors with high turnover to ensure food freshness.
3. Restaurant Hygiene: Choose reputable restaurants, especially those with good

reviews, to minimize the risk of foodborne illnesses. If you have a sensitive stomach, consider eating in more established, well-known establishments.

Naples is a vibrant, historic city with much to offer visitors, and while there are a few safety considerations to keep in mind, it is generally a safe and welcoming destination. By taking standard precautions, such as safeguarding your belongings, being mindful of your surroundings, and following health guidelines, you can have an enjoyable and safe trip to this beautiful city.

BUDGETING AND CURRENCY TIPS

When visiting Naples, budgeting wisely and understanding the currency system are key to ensuring a smooth and enjoyable experience. Italy uses the Euro (EUR), and there are several ways to manage your expenses effectively while exploring the city.

- Currency and Exchange Rates

The currency used in Naples is the Euro (EUR), which is also the official currency of Italy. Before traveling, it's a good idea to check the current exchange rates if you're coming from a country that uses a different currency. You can exchange money at banks, exchange offices, or withdraw Euros from ATMs once you arrive in Naples.

1. ATMs: ATMs are widely available throughout Naples, including near tourist attractions, airports, and train stations. They typically offer competitive exchange rates. However, be mindful of potential ATM fees, which may be charged by your bank, especially for international withdrawals. It's recommended to use ATMs associated with well-known banks to avoid issues.

2. Currency Exchange: Currency exchange services can be found at Naples' central

stations, the airport, and in tourist areas. While convenient, these services often offer less favorable rates and may charge commission fees. If possible, it's better to exchange money at banks or use ATMs for better rates.

3. Credit and Debit Cards: Credit and debit cards are widely accepted in Naples, especially in restaurants, hotels, and shops. However, it's still advisable to carry some cash for smaller establishments, markets, and in case of emergencies. Major international cards like Visa and Mastercard are commonly used, while American Express is less widely accepted.

- Budgeting Tips for Naples

Naples is known for offering a variety of experiences to fit different budgets. Whether you're looking for affordable street food or enjoying fine dining, there are options to suit every price range.

1. Accommodation: Naples has a wide range of accommodation options, from budget hostels and guesthouses to mid-range hotels and luxury resorts. For those traveling on a budget, consider staying in areas like Vomero, Materdei, or near the Central Train Station, where prices are lower, and you'll find affordable hostels, guesthouses, and small hotels. Booking in advance is often a good way to secure better rates, particularly in peak tourist seasons.

2. Dining: Naples is famous for its pizza, and you can find delicious, affordable pizza in many local pizzerias. Pizza Margherita, which originated in Naples, can be enjoyed for as little as €5-€8 at many casual pizzerias. Street food such as sfogliatella, a traditional pastry, or pizza margherita by the slice, can

also be very budget-friendly. For a sit-down meal, expect to pay between €15-€30 for a main course, depending on the restaurant and location. Fine dining establishments, especially near the coast, will be more expensive, with meals ranging from €40-€70 per person.

3. Transportation: Public transportation in Naples is affordable. A single metro or bus ticket costs about €1.30, while day passes for unlimited travel can be purchased for around €4-€5. If you're planning to visit multiple attractions, consider purchasing a Naples City Pass or any special tourist passes that offer discounts for multiple attractions, public transport, and museums.

4. Attractions and Sightseeing: Naples offers a mix of free and paid attractions. The historic center is free to explore, and walking around areas like Spaccanapoli or visiting Piazza del

Plebiscito doesn't cost anything. Major attractions, such as the Naples National Archaeological Museum or the Royal Palace, typically charge an entrance fee of around €10-€15. Discounts or free entry days are often available for students, EU residents, or during special events, so it's worth checking before your visit.

5. Souvenirs and Shopping: Naples is known for its artisan shops, selling everything from ceramics to leather goods. If you're looking for budget-friendly souvenirs, you can find small trinkets, magnets, or local food products at affordable prices in local markets or from street vendors. Artisan shops may be a bit pricier, but their high-quality products can still be reasonable if you're looking for something special to take home.

- Tipping

Tipping in Naples is not as mandatory or expected as in some other countries, but it's appreciated for good service. In restaurants, a service charge of around 10% is often included in the bill, but it's common to leave a small additional tip for excellent service, such as rounding up the bill or leaving €1-€2 for smaller meals. For taxis, rounding up to the nearest Euro or leaving a €1-€2 tip is typical. Porters and hotel staff may also appreciate small tips for their assistance.

- Cost-Saving Tips

To make your budget go further in Naples, consider the following:

1. Visit free attractions: Naples has many free things to see, such as the historic center, Piazza del Plebiscito, San Gregorio Armeno, and even wandering the streets of the Spanish Quarter or the waterfront.

2. Buy groceries or snacks: To save on meals, consider buying fresh food from local markets like Mercato di Porta Nolana or Mercato di Pignasecca, where you can pick up local products such as bread, cheese, fruits, and meats for a picnic or to cook your own meals.

3. Take advantage of lunch specials: Many restaurants offer menu del giorno (daily menu) options during lunch hours that provide a full meal at a discounted price. These typically include a starter, main course, and sometimes dessert or coffee, making it a great way to enjoy a good meal without breaking the bank.

4. Consider walking or using public transport: Naples is a walkable city, and many of its top attractions are located close to each other. Save money on transportation by exploring

on foot. If you need to take public transport, it's cheap and reliable.

Naples is a city that offers options for all types of budgets, from budget travelers seeking affordable food and accommodation to those looking to indulge in luxury experiences. With a bit of planning and flexibility, it's possible to enjoy all that this vibrant city has to offer without overspending. Keep an eye on your spending, use cash wisely, and take advantage of the many affordable dining and sightseeing opportunities to make the most of your trip.

NAVIGATING NAPLES AS A SOLO TRAVELER

Navigating Naples as a solo traveler can be a rewarding experience, offering opportunities for personal exploration, cultural immersion, and the freedom to move at your own pace. While the city has a reputation for being a bit chaotic, it's also welcoming and vibrant, with a rich history, beautiful scenery, and a distinct atmosphere that's perfect for solo adventurers. Here are some tips to help you make the most of your solo journey through Naples.

- Staying Safe as a Solo Traveler

Naples is generally safe for solo travelers, but like any major city, it's important to stay vigilant. Here are some safety tips to help you navigate the city with confidence:

1. Stay in Well-Trodden Areas: Stick to popular and well-lit areas, particularly in the evenings. The historic center, Piazza del Plebiscito, Spaccanapoli, and the waterfront are all busy, safe, and ideal for solo exploration. Avoid walking alone in darker or quieter neighborhoods late at night, particularly in areas like Scampia or Secondigliano, which are known for higher crime rates.

2. Keep Your Belongings Secure: Petty theft, such as pickpocketing, is common in crowded areas, especially around major tourist spots and public transport. Always keep your bag close to you, and use anti-theft bags or money belts to protect your valuables. Be especially cautious on public transportation and when in busy markets.

3. Trust Your Instincts: If you ever feel uncomfortable in a situation or a location, don't hesitate to leave. Naples is a friendly city, but if something doesn't feel right, it's always better to err on the side of caution.

- Getting Around Naples

Navigating Naples as a solo traveler is straightforward, as the city offers several options for transport. It's a walkable city, and public transport is efficient and affordable.

1. Walking: Naples is a very walkable city, especially in the historic center where most of the main attractions are located within walking distance. Walking through the narrow streets of the Spanish Quarter or along the waterfront is a fantastic way to immerse yourself in the city's atmosphere. Just be mindful of traffic—Neapolitan drivers can be a bit unpredictable, so always look both ways when crossing the street.

2. Public Transport: Naples has an extensive and affordable public transport system, including buses, metro lines, and funiculars. A single metro or bus ticket costs around €1.30, and you can buy day passes or multi-ride tickets for savings. The metro system is fairly straightforward and can take you to most of the city's main tourist sites. The funiculars, which connect the city center to the hilltop neighborhoods of Vomero and Posillipo, are also convenient for solo

travelers looking to enjoy panoramic views of the city.

3. Taxis and Ride-Sharing: Taxis are widely available but can be expensive. Solo travelers might find ride-sharing apps like Uber or FreeNow to be more convenient and cost-effective for shorter trips.

- Connecting with Locals

One of the best ways to experience Naples as a solo traveler is to connect with locals. Neapolitans are known for their warmth and hospitality, and you'll often find that people are more than happy to help you.

1. Language: While Italian is the official language, many people, especially those in tourist areas, speak basic English. Learning a few key phrases in Italian, like "Ciao" (hello) or "Grazie" (thank you), can go a long way in establishing rapport with locals.

2. Cafés and Restaurants: Naples has a vibrant café culture, and sitting in one of the city's many cafés, such as those around Piazza del Plebiscito or the Lungomare, can be a great way to people-watch and connect with locals. Enjoying a coffee at the bar is a great social experience, even if you're on your own. Don't be afraid to strike up conversations with baristas or fellow patrons—many Neapolitans are eager to chat.

3. Tours and Activities: Joining group tours or activities can be a great way to meet other solo travelers and engage with locals. Consider booking a walking tour of the historic center, a pizza-making class, or a guided hike up Mount Vesuvius. Many local guides are passionate about sharing the history and culture of the city, and these tours provide opportunities to meet others while discovering hidden gems.

- Solo Dining

Dining solo in Naples is an enjoyable experience. The city is known for its pizza, and there are countless pizzerias where you can comfortably eat alone. Many restaurants have cozy, single-person tables, and it's common to see locals eating solo, especially during lunch or a mid-afternoon break.

1. Pizza: Naples is the birthplace of pizza, and a solo pizza meal is one of the most iconic experiences you can have. You'll find pizzerias throughout the city, with many serving delicious Margherita pizza for around €5-€8. If you're looking for something more, try other local specialties like pizza marinara or sfogliatella for dessert.

2. Cafés and Bars: Naples has a rich café culture, and sitting at a counter or table for a quick espresso or pastry is common. Cafés such as Caffè Gambrinus near Piazza del

Plebiscito or Gran Caffè La Caffettiera offer a great place to relax and enjoy a coffee or a snack.

3. Markets: If you're a fan of fresh, local food, visit one of Naples' markets, like Mercato di Porta Nolana or Mercato di Pignasecca, to sample street food and buy local products. Markets are great for solo travelers because they provide an authentic experience, and you can easily wander and explore at your own pace.

- Solo-Friendly Activities

There are plenty of solo-friendly activities in Naples, from cultural experiences to natural exploration.

1. Museums and Historical Sites: Naples is home to numerous fascinating museums, including the Naples National Archaeological Museum, the Capodimonte

Museum, and the historic Castel dell'Ovo. These places offer an enriching solo experience where you can immerse yourself in art and history at your own pace.

2. Mount Vesuvius: Hiking Mount Vesuvius is an exciting and rewarding solo adventure. The hike to the summit offers spectacular views of the city and the Bay of Naples, and it's a great way to connect with nature while experiencing a piece of history.

3. Beaches and Coastal Walks: Naples has access to stunning coastal areas, including the Lungomare promenade, which offers fantastic views of the Gulf of Naples. You can also take a short trip to the nearby Posillipo Hill or visit beaches like Bagno Elena. These areas are ideal for solo travelers looking to enjoy some quiet time by the water.

Naples is a fantastic city for solo travelers, offering a mix of cultural immersion, local charm, and the freedom to explore at your own pace. With its welcoming locals, safe areas to explore, and a wealth of activities suited for individuals, Naples presents a perfect destination for those looking to experience Italy's history, cuisine, and natural beauty in a personal and enriching way. Whether you're wandering through narrow streets, enjoying a meal, or embarking on an adventure, Naples will provide plenty of opportunities to create unforgettable memories as a solo traveler.

ESSENTIAL APPS AND RESOURCES

When traveling solo in Naples, having the right apps and resources at your fingertips can significantly enhance your experience, making it easier to navigate the city, discover new places, and manage your trip. Here's a list of essential apps and resources to help you make the most of your journey.

For navigation and transportation, Google Maps is indispensable. It provides clear directions, whether you're walking, taking public transport, or driving, and includes real-time updates. Moovit is another great option for navigating Naples' public transport system, helping you find the quickest routes for buses, metros, and funiculars. For a more local experience, the Napoli Mobilità app offers details about public transport schedules and routes, as well as the ability to purchase tickets directly through the app. Additionally, for ridesharing, Free Now (formerly MyTaxi) is a reliable option in Naples, allowing you to easily hail a taxi or private ride.

Language and translation apps are also crucial for solo travelers. Google Translate is an essential tool for overcoming language barriers, allowing you to translate menus, signs, and conversations in real time. Duolingo is perfect for learning basic Italian phrases before your trip, which can make your interactions with locals more enjoyable.

To help plan your sightseeing, TripAdvisor is a fantastic app for finding top-rated attractions, restaurants, and hotels based on real reviews from other travelers. TheFork is a useful app for discovering and booking restaurants in Naples, offering discounts and reservations. For booking tours and activities, GetYourGuide is an excellent resource, offering a wide variety of experiences like guided walking tours or tickets to popular sights such as the Naples National Archaeological Museum or Pompeii.

If you're looking to connect with locals or other travelers, Eventbrite provides listings for local events, concerts, and exhibitions happening during your visit. Meetup is also an excellent app for joining local groups or activities, whether you're interested in hiking, language exchange, or food tours.

For managing finances, Revolut is a must-have for solo travelers. It allows you to manage multiple currencies with low exchange rates and no hidden fees. XE Currency is another great tool for tracking exchange rates in real time, so you can stay on top of how much you're spending in euros. If you prefer to eat in, Just Eat and Uber Eats are convenient apps for ordering food from local restaurants, whether you're craving a pizza or traditional Neapolitan pastries.

Staying prepared for any situation is important, and apps like The Weather Channel are great for checking the weather during your trip, so you can plan your outings accordingly. In case of an emergency, 112 is the European Union's emergency number, and it's advisable to have the First Aid by American Red Cross app on hand for guidance on handling medical issues while traveling.

Lastly, for those looking to explore the city in depth, the Naples City Pass app offers discounted entry to major museums, galleries, and historic sites, helping you save money on tickets. The Naples Map and Walks app provides self-guided tours, allowing you to explore neighborhoods, art, and history at your own pace.

Having these essential apps and resources will make navigating Naples, finding the best experiences, and staying safe during your solo adventure a breeze. Whether you need to get around, find the best food, or book activities, these tools will help ensure your trip is smooth, enjoyable, and unforgettable.

CHAPTER TWELVE

NAPLES IN 2025: WHAT'S NEW?

UPCOMING EVENTS AND FESTIVALS

Naples is a city that's alive with energy year-round, and it hosts a variety of events and festivals that showcase its rich culture, history, and vibrant traditions. Whether you're visiting for a short time or an extended stay, there's always something exciting happening. Here's a look at some of the key upcoming events and festivals in Naples in 2025.

- Naples Carnival (Carnival of Naples)

Carnival season in Naples is a lively time, usually taking place in February. The city celebrates with colorful parades, street performances, and local traditions. Expect vibrant costumes, music, and food stalls, as well as theatrical performances that depict the city's historical figures and folklore. The Vico San Gregorio Armeno, famous for its nativity scene workshops, also comes alive during the Carnival, with artisans showcasing their skills and celebrating the season.

- Easter Week Celebrations (Settimana Santa)

Easter is a significant religious event in Naples, and the city holds impressive religious processions throughout Holy Week (Settimana Santa), leading up to Easter Sunday. The most iconic is the Processione dei Misteri (Procession of the Mysteries), a solemn event with participants dressed in traditional costumes, walking through the narrow streets of the historic center. If you're visiting in spring, this is a deeply moving cultural experience, combining faith, tradition, and Naples' unique charm.

- Naples Pizza Village

Held in late spring (typically in May or June), the Naples Pizza Village is a food lover's paradise, celebrating the city's most famous dish pizza. Located along the Lungomare (waterfront), the event features pizza makers from around the world, cooking up traditional Neapolitan pizzas. Visitors can sample different styles of pizza, attend cooking demonstrations, and participate in pizza-making workshops. It's a fantastic event for anyone wanting to dive into Naples' culinary culture.

- Festival of San Gennaro

One of the most important religious celebrations in Naples, the Feast of San Gennaro, takes place every year on September 19th. San Gennaro is the patron saint of Naples, and this day is marked by religious ceremonies, processions, and events across the city. The highlight is the liquefaction of the blood of San Gennaro, a miraculous event believed to bring prosperity to the city. The streets around Duomo di San Gennaro fill with visitors and worshippers, and the celebrations are accompanied by concerts and public gatherings.

- Naples Jazz Festival

If you're a music lover, the Naples Jazz Festival is a must-see. Held in June, the festival brings together international jazz artists and local talents for a series of performances. The festival takes place at various venues across the city, including open-air stages, theaters, and jazz clubs. It's a great way to experience Naples' lively music scene and enjoy world-class performances in intimate settings.

- Naples Film Festival

For cinema enthusiasts, the Naples Film Festival (usually held in October) is a celebration of both Italian and international cinema. The event showcases a diverse selection of films, from independent productions to international blockbusters, as well as documentaries and short films. The festival includes screenings at multiple venues, often accompanied by Q&A sessions with filmmakers and actors, making it an exciting event for those interested in film culture.

- Christmas Markets and Festivities

Naples is famous for its festive atmosphere during the Christmas season. From late November through December, the city is decorated with sparkling lights and the streets bustle with holiday activity. One of the most iconic places to visit during this time is Via San Gregorio Armeno, where you can shop for traditional Neapolitan nativity figurines and handmade decorations. Piazza del Plebiscito and Spaccanapoli are also home to Christmas markets selling food, local crafts, and gifts. Naples' Christmas season also features performances, concerts, and the annual New Year's Eve celebrations in the city center, with fireworks and live music.

- Vesuvius Wine Festival

For wine enthusiasts, the Vesuvius Wine Festival (held in October) is a celebration of the region's wine culture. Held at the foot of Mount Vesuvius, this event offers wine tastings from local wineries, food pairings, and the chance to learn about the wine production process in this volcanic region. The festival highlights the unique wines made from grapes grown in the fertile volcanic soil around the mountain, particularly the Lacryma Christi variety.

- Naples Theatre Season

Throughout the year, Naples has a rich theatre scene, with performances ranging from classic Italian plays to contemporary works. The Teatro di San Carlo, one of the most famous opera houses in Italy, offers a full calendar of opera, ballet, and classical music performances. Additionally, there are a variety of smaller venues hosting plays, comedy shows, and experimental theatre throughout the year. If you're visiting Naples, it's worth checking the local listings to see what's on during your stay.

- La Giornata Nazionale delle Ferrovie Dimenticate (National Day of Forgotten Railways)

This annual event, typically held in April or May, celebrates the unique and historic train routes that were once part of Italy's railway system but are now no longer in operation. While not as large as other festivals, this event is a fun and offbeat way to explore the countryside around Naples, especially if you're interested in history and vintage trains.

Naples is full of exciting events and festivals throughout the year, with something for everyone whether you're interested in food, music, history, or religious traditions. From the world-famous Naples Pizza Village to the cultural richness of Easter and the Festival of San Gennaro, there's no shortage of experiences that can make your visit even more memorable. Check local event calendars closer to your travel dates to ensure you don't miss out on any unique celebrations during your stay.

EMERGING TRAVEL TRENDS

In recent years, travel trends have evolved significantly, and Naples, with its unique blend of history, culture, and modern attractions, is benefiting from several emerging travel trends. As we look toward 2025, here are some key travel trends that are likely to shape the way visitors explore Naples and the surrounding region.

- Sustainable Travel and Eco-Tourism

As environmental awareness grows, more travelers are opting for sustainable and eco-friendly travel experiences. In Naples, this trend is reflected in the rise of green hotels, eco-conscious restaurants, and sustainable transportation options. Travelers are increasingly seeking ways to minimize their carbon footprint by opting for eco-friendly modes of transport such as electric scooters, hybrid cars, or public transportation. Many travelers are also interested in exploring natural attractions like Vesuvius National Park and the Amalfi Coast in a responsible way, focusing on preserving these unique environments. In addition, there is a growing demand for eco-tours, where travelers can explore the region's rich biodiversity and participate in conservation efforts.

- Cultural and Authentic Travel

Travelers are increasingly prioritizing authentic and immersive cultural experiences over traditional sightseeing. In Naples, this means exploring the city's vibrant neighborhoods, interacting with locals, and discovering hidden gems that aren't part of the typical tourist itinerary. From San Gregorio Armeno and its artisan shops to attending local festivals like the

Naples Pizza Village, travelers want to experience the real life of the city. Visitors are also seeking deeper connections with local traditions, such as cooking classes, street food tours, and learning the art of making authentic Neapolitan pizza or sfogliatella.

- Solo Travel and Female Empowerment

Solo travel continues to rise in popularity, especially among women. Naples, with its rich cultural history, welcoming locals, and walkable city center, is an ideal destination for solo travelers. The city offers a mix of safe, quiet neighborhoods and bustling areas with plenty of cafes, museums, and local attractions to explore. For female travelers, solo trips to Naples are increasingly common, with the city's vibrant café culture, numerous cultural events, and easy-to-navigate streets making it a comfortable destination. More solo travelers are also looking for off-the-beaten-path experiences, such as exploring Pompeii or hiking up Mount Vesuvius on their own terms.

- Digital Nomadism and Workations

As remote work becomes a permanent fixture for many professionals, digital nomadism is a trend that's gaining ground. Naples, with its affordable cost of living compared to other European cities, beautiful surroundings, and robust internet infrastructure, is becoming an attractive location for remote workers seeking a change of scenery. Many digital nomads are choosing to live and work in Naples for a few months, combining their professional responsibilities with opportunities to explore the city's rich cultural offerings, from museums and art galleries to its culinary delights. Workations, where travelers mix work and vacation, are also on the rise, with many seeking out accommodations that offer both comfort and business amenities, such as high-speed internet and quiet spaces for video calls.

- Local Experiences and Customization

There is a growing desire among travelers to enjoy more personalized and tailored travel experiences. In Naples, this trend manifests in bespoke tours and experiences that cater to individual interests. Whether it's a private tour of Pompeii with a local archaeologist, a cooking class with a Neapolitan chef, or a boat tour around Naples Bay and the Amalfi Coast, travelers want to create their own unique itineraries. Many are opting for private, customized experiences that allow them to dive deeper into the culture, food, and history of the region.

- Health and Wellness Tourism

The global rise in wellness tourism is influencing travel choices in Naples as well. Travelers are seeking destinations that offer not only relaxation but also health-focused experiences. Naples, with its natural thermal baths, proximity to healing volcanic areas, and an increasing number of wellness hotels, is becoming a destination for those looking to rejuvenate both physically and mentally. Visitors are booking wellness retreats, engaging in hiking and yoga sessions on the slopes of Mount Vesuvius, or enjoying spa treatments at local resorts. The city's mild Mediterranean climate, especially during the spring and autumn months, also makes it a great destination for outdoor activities like cycling, hiking, and beach wellness.

- Food Tourism and Culinary Travel

Food continues to be one of the most significant reasons people travel, and Naples, as the birthplace of pizza, is perfectly situated to take advantage of this trend. Beyond pizza, the city offers a rich culinary heritage, and more tourists are traveling to Naples specifically to discover its gastronomic delights. From indulging in local street food like sfogliatella and pizza margherita to experiencing fine dining, food tourism in Naples is growing. Travelers are seeking unique food experiences such as private pizza-making classes, culinary tours, and wine tastings of local wines like Lacryma Christi from the slopes of Vesuvius. This trend also includes a growing interest in regional specialties, such as pasta alla Genovese and limoncello.

- Adventure and Active Travel

More travelers are seeking adventure and physical activity as part of their holidays, and Naples, with its stunning landscapes and natural beauty, is an ideal destination for adventure tourism. Hiking Mount Vesuvius, exploring the Amalfi Coast by bike, or kayaking in Naples Bay are just some of the active travel experiences that are growing in popularity. In addition, Naples offers opportunities for diving, sailing, and rock climbing, particularly in the scenic areas surrounding the city, such as Capri, Ischia, and Procida. Adventure travelers are increasingly drawn to the unique combination of nature, history, and adventure that Naples offers.

- Technology and Smart Tourism

Naples is embracing the future with the integration of technology into the tourism experience. Smart tourism is becoming more prominent, with tech tools that help visitors navigate the city and discover hidden gems. Digital guides, augmented reality apps, and online booking platforms are making it easier than ever for travelers to find personalized experiences. Apps that allow for contactless payments, digital tickets to attractions, and virtual museum tours are becoming common, allowing visitors to explore the city in a more convenient and modern way. The integration of these technologies enhances the visitor experience and reflects the growing demand for more seamless travel experiences.

As we look ahead to 2025, Naples is poised to welcome travelers from around the world, embracing emerging trends that highlight sustainability, authenticity, health, and personalization. Whether you're a solo traveler seeking local experiences, a digital nomad looking for a mix of work and leisure, or a food lover eager to indulge in the city's culinary offerings, Naples offers something for everyone. These emerging trends reflect the changing landscape of travel and Naples' ability to adapt and offer enriching, memorable experiences to all its visitors.

SUSTAINABILITY AND ECO-TOURISM

Sustainability and eco-tourism are becoming central to travel, with an increasing number of travelers seeking ways to explore the world responsibly while minimizing their environmental impact. Naples, with its rich natural landscapes, cultural heritage, and emerging eco-conscious initiatives, is embracing sustainable travel to preserve its beauty for future generations. From green accommodations to nature-friendly excursions, the city and its surrounding regions offer numerous opportunities for travelers who value sustainability and environmental stewardship.

Naples is home to an increasing number of eco-friendly hotels and accommodations that focus on reducing their carbon footprint. Many boutique hotels and larger establishments are adopting sustainable practices such as energy-efficient lighting, water conservation, plastic reduction, and sourcing local, organic food for their guests. Some accommodations now provide bike rentals, encourage public transportation use, and support local artisans by showcasing their work. For travelers, staying in eco-conscious accommodations contributes to responsible tourism and helps support local businesses.

One of the key eco-tourism draws in the Naples region is Mount Vesuvius National Park. This stunning volcanic landscape, which is both historically significant and ecologically diverse, offers visitors the chance to explore nature responsibly. Visitors can hike sustainable trails, learn about the area's biodiversity, and admire breathtaking views of the Gulf of Naples. Local guides often lead tours focused on conservation and education, highlighting the need to preserve the unique environment around the volcano.

Another natural gem is the nearby Amalfi Coast, a UNESCO World Heritage Site known for its dramatic cliffs, crystal-clear waters, and charming villages. Eco-conscious travelers can explore the area on foot by walking along ancient hiking trails, such as the Path of the Gods (Sentiero degli Dei), which provide sweeping views without harming the environment. Boat tours now also promote sustainable practices, including electric boats that reduce pollution in the fragile coastal waters. Many visitors opt for low-impact transportation, such as ferries and public buses, to navigate the coastal towns instead of renting private cars.

Sustainable agriculture and eco-conscious food production are also integral to the Naples region. Visitors can explore organic farms and vineyards around the slopes of Vesuvius, where traditional farming techniques are still practiced. Many wineries offer eco-tours, allowing visitors to taste local wines like Lacryma Christi while learning about organic winemaking and the importance of sustainable agriculture. Farm-to-table experiences are growing in popularity, where travelers can savor meals made with fresh, seasonal produce sourced locally.

Naples also encourages eco-conscious transportation options to reduce carbon emissions in the city. The expansion of bike-sharing programs, the promotion of electric scooters, and improvements to the city's metro and bus networks make it easier for travelers to move around in a sustainable way. Walking remains one of the best ways to explore Naples, especially in areas like the Historic Center or along the scenic Lungomare, where visitors can enjoy car-free zones and reduce their environmental footprint.

Local markets, such as the Pignasecca Market, offer another way to engage in sustainable tourism. By shopping at local markets, travelers support small businesses and artisans while reducing the demand for mass-produced goods. Markets in Naples emphasize fresh, local produce and handmade crafts, providing travelers with a more authentic and environmentally friendly shopping experience.

For those seeking immersive eco-experiences, marine conservation tours and volunteer opportunities are available around Naples' coastal waters and islands like Capri and Ischia. These tours often involve beach cleanups, marine life education, and sustainable snorkeling or diving excursions that emphasize the importance of protecting marine ecosystems. Conservation groups and responsible tour operators play a key role in educating visitors on preserving the fragile marine habitats of the Gulf of Naples.

Another area of focus is the promotion of cultural sustainability, where travelers are encouraged to support local traditions, artisans, and small businesses. Workshops on crafts like pottery, nativity figurine making, and traditional Neapolitan cooking allow visitors to connect with Naples' cultural heritage while supporting its continuation. By choosing authentic experiences, travelers help sustain the local economy and ensure that these traditions thrive for years to come.

Naples is also making strides in waste management and reducing plastic use, particularly in tourist-heavy areas. Restaurants and cafes are increasingly adopting biodegradable packaging and reducing single-use plastics, while campaigns promote reusable water bottles and refill stations around the city. Conscious travelers are encouraged to participate in these efforts by minimizing waste, avoiding plastic, and recycling whenever possible.

Finally, educational eco-tours and experiences are on the rise, combining tourism with conservation. Visitors can participate in guided tours that teach them about Naples' environment, history, and efforts to address sustainability challenges. Whether exploring ancient Roman ruins or hiking through protected parks, travelers can gain a greater understanding of the need for preservation while enjoying their visit responsibly.

Sustainability and eco-tourism are more than trends; they are part of a larger movement toward conscious travel. Naples, with its natural beauty, rich culture, and emerging green initiatives, offers an ideal destination for those who seek to travel responsibly. By supporting local businesses, embracing sustainable transportation, and exploring the city's natural landscapes in an eco-friendly way, visitors can play a part in preserving Naples' timeless charm while enjoying a truly meaningful travel experience.

ACKNOWLEGDEMENT

ABOUT THE AUTHOR

Aria Wild is a passionate traveler, writer, and storyteller dedicated to inspiring others to explore the world and immerse themselves in diverse cultures. With a background in journalism and a lifelong curiosity about different ways of life, Aria has made it her mission to uncover the stories that make each destination unique.

Her love for travel began at an early age, sparked by family road trips and later nurtured through solo adventures to far-flung corners of the globe. Over the years, she has journeyed through bustling cities, serene countryside, and remote islands, documenting her experiences through vivid narratives and compelling photography.

Aria specializes in creating practical yet immersive travel guides designed to help readers connect deeply with the places they visit. She blends firsthand knowledge with a flair for uncovering hidden gems, ensuring her work resonates with both seasoned globetrotters and first-time travelers.

In addition to writing, Aria advocates for sustainable and responsible tourism. She believes in the importance of supporting local communities, preserving cultural heritage, and protecting the natural environment, and her work often highlights ways travelers can make a positive impact.

When she's not traveling, Aria enjoys hiking, experimenting with recipes from around the world, and indulging in her love for literature and art. She finds inspiration in the connections she forges with people and places, and she brings this sense of wonder and discovery to her writing.

Through her travel guides and essays, Aria Wild invites readers to see the world not just as tourists but as explorers with an open heart and mind, ready to embrace the beauty and complexity of the global tapestry.

HAPPY TRAVEL

Made in United States
Cleveland, OH
07 March 2025